Wendy Stacey is t ... the Mayo School of Astrology, and a tutor for the London School of Astrology. She is Chair of the Astrological Association of Great Britain and writes a regular student feature in its publication, *The Astrological Journal*. Wendy has also written *Consulting with Astrology: A Quick Guide to Building Your Practice and Profile*.

First published in 2012
by The Mayo Press in association with Flare Publications
The Mayo, BCM Box 175, London, WC1N 3XX
Website: www.mayoastrology.com
Email: enquiries@mayoastrology.com

A CIP catalogue record for this book is available
from the British Library

ISBN: 978-1-903353-28-8

Cover: Cat Keane

Layout and formatting:
Frank Clifford (second printing), Craig Knottenbelt (first printing)

Text editing and proofing:
Jane Struthers, Alice Ekrek, Caroline Moroz, Frank Clifford

Data verification: Sy Scholfield, www.syscholfield.com

WENDY STACEY

URANUS
SQUARE
PLUTO

For Marj

– my grandmother, a double Virgo,
and my greatest inspiration,
who died while I was writing this book.

Acknowledgements

Thank you to Nick Campion and Frank Clifford for their excellent data resources. To Sy Scholfield for so efficiently verifying the data in this book. To the text editors, Alice Ekrek, my good friend and peer who is always such a delight to work with and has a great eye for detail; and Jane Struthers who did a wonderful job and whose editing skills are truly second to none. Thank you to my dear friend and colleague, Caroline Moroz, who did some proofing on this book during such a challenging time in her life, and for this I am extremely grateful.

Thank you to Craig Knottenbelt for his patience and great care that he took with this book and to one of my closest friends and one of the best artists I know, Cat Keane, who always intuitively knows what you want and has the wisdom to know what will work, thank you for designing the cover of this book.

Thank you to my colleagues Roy Gillett and Sue Tompkins for lecturing on this topic with me for the Mayo School's *Uranus–Pluto Square* online conference, and to the family, friends and colleagues who have supported the project along the way. I would also like to take this opportunity to honour my good and long-time friend Peter Adcock-White whose vision, wisdom and words are just so incredibly beautiful.

Finally, I would like to extend my gratitude to four people whose contribution words could never describe. Firstly, to Frank Clifford, whose guidance, support, motivation, intelligence and friendship have been invaluable through every single step of this project. And to my husband Amin and daughters Seline and Zahra, who have been so exceptionally tolerant, patient, understanding, supportive and encouraging throughout the project, and whom I love very much.

Contents

Preface   11

Introduction   13

Uranus Meets Pluto   17
  • The Uranus–Pluto Cycle   19
  • The Uranus–Pluto Conjunction 1965–66   27
  • The Uranus–Pluto Sextile 1995–97   37
  • The Uranus–Pluto Square 1932–34   39

The Uranus–Pluto Landscape of Today   43
  • The Ingress of Pluto into Capricorn   45
  • The Ingress of Uranus into Aries   55
  • The Cardinal Climax   63
  • The Meltdown and Firing Up of Iceland   79
  • Riots Rooted in Inequality   87
      – The London Riots   87
      – The Civil Rights Movement and
        Martin Luther King   88
      – The Watts Riots   90
      – South Africa and Nelson Mandela   90
      – The LA Riots and Rodney King   94
  • A Vision of the Near Future   101
      – Economic Failings, Aftershocks and
        Changes   101
      – Threat of Pandemics   104
      – Interesting Dates   106
      – Beyond 2020   109

Back to the Future – Towards a Virgo Society   111
  • Virgo Characteristics and the Maiden   113
  • Work   117
  • Health   123
  • Industry   135

  • Research, Methods and Data Collection   141
  • Witchcraft   143
  • Fashion, Trends and Pop Culture   149

Other Current Planetary Cycles   **159**
  • The Jupiter–Saturn Cycle   161
  • The Jupiter–Uranus Cycle   167
  • The Jupiter–Pluto Cycle   175
  • The Saturn–Uranus Cycle   177
  • The Saturn–Pluto Cycle   179
  • The Ingress of Neptune into Pisces   181
  • Uranus and Neptune in Mutual Reception   193
  • Chiron and Mundane Astrology   197

The Personal is Political   **203**

Conclusion   **207**

Appendix   **210**
  • Astrology Symbol Keys   210
  • Hard Aspects and Ingresses of Jupiter,
    Saturn, Chiron, Uranus, Neptune and
    Pluto, 2007–15   212
  • Uranus–Pluto Aspects 1850–2104   215

Bibliography   218
Birth Data   223
About the Author   230
About the Mayo School of Astrology   232

Index   **237**

All charts in this book have been calculated using the Placidus house system, Chiron and the five Ptolemaic aspects.

Preface

This book started accidently when I was asked to deliver the Carter Memorial Lecture for the 2011 Astrological Association Conference in the UK. It was an honour to be invited to give this prestigious lecture and speakers are given two years to prepare for it. It is usually based on the presenter's life work or a subject close to their heart. Given the economic collapse that was occurring at the time and watching so many people around me – friends, family and clients – become casualties of the looming recession, it didn't take long to decide on the subject of my presentation: the Uranus–Pluto squares that would become exact between 2012 and 2015, but were already being felt through the introduction of other planetary phenomena.

Uranus and Pluto travelled through Virgo for most of the 1960s and I was born in this era and therefore have Uranus and Pluto conjunct in Virgo in my own horoscope (as well as Jupiter in Virgo in the sixth house). The conjunction of Uranus and Pluto straddles my Descendant, which perhaps explains why I have a strong desire to write about this particular subject and also why my research for the Carter Memorial Lecture just kept expanding. The biggest obstacle I encountered in writing this book was wrapping it up, as so many relevant events occurred daily – and these continue to unfold.

Another challenge in writing this book was to put the information into a coherent and systematic structure as there is so much to take into account. This book is about the Uranus–Pluto squares and how they are relevant to our present society. However, as astrologers we know that cycles cannot be analysed in isolation; while interpreting the cycle we must take into account all the other cycles and ingresses which are also taking place. Over recent years there have been many, and these have been included and discussed in this book.

I would like to thank Michael Baigent, Nicholas Campion and Charles Harvey for their book *Mundane Astrology: An Introduction to the Astrology of Nations and Groups*. Their contribution to mundane astrology has led the way for so many astrologers (including myself) to continue research in this field. It is a shame that Charles Harvey was taken so early in his life, as there was so much more we could have learnt from him. A personal thank you to Nicholas Campion, whose book, *The Book of World Horoscopes*, is an invaluable, rigorous collection of data and research. I look forward to the translated works of Andre Barbault, the French mundane astrologer, whom I am sure will bestow further insight, wisdom and guidance for future mundane research.

Introduction

The area of mundane astrology is a fascinating one. Most astrology is practised or studied from a natal perspective, looking at the astrological information and how this pertains to somebody's personality, character traits and potential. The natal chart describes the individual's life journey, the timing of events and the decisions they will be faced with throughout their life. As astrologers we also acknowledge free will and understand that people have choices. Therefore, we cannot tell an individual exactly what will happen but we can provide guidance on the themes that they will encounter at particular times in their lives.

Mundane astrology uses the same astrological signatures, but here we extend the interpretation not to the individual but to the social, political and economic. Using mundane astrology we can explore the outer planetary cycles and observe how, from a sociological perspective, the astrological themes relate to a particular era. The planetary configurations tell the story not just of the individual but also of history and social change. As the cycles of the planets continue their journeys through the solar system, their positions in the zodiac and the aspects they make to each other are mirrored in our own collective unconscious – as above, so below. We are reminded by Nick Campion that planetary cycles do not cause events to happen, but their cycles are markers of time and these represent or reflect the events on Earth.[1]

When Uranus and Pluto came to conjunction in the 1960s, a new era and generation was born. It spearheaded radical social, economic and political reform. The generation born at

---

1. Nicholas Campion, 'Revolutionary Years and the Uranus–Pluto Cycle', *The Mountain Astrologer*, Aug/Sep 2011, Issue 158, p. 32.

this time has now reached its 40s and 50s and is living through the challenges that the cardinal Uranus–Pluto square brings. Its members are also responsible for steering the challenges, crises and opportunities that the current cardinal Uranus–Pluto square presents.

The book refers back to the 1960s conjunction and those born of it, what it carries with it, what it seeks to change and achieve, and possible areas of challenge – along with the current astrological climate (for instance, Uranus in Aries and Neptune in Pisces). The aim of this book is to discuss the Uranus–Pluto cycle from a mundane perspective while looking at it through a magnifying glass and attempting to put it into an astrological framework that is relevant to our era as both astrologers and as members of society.

Between 2008 and 2015 several outer planetary aspects occur (an appendix is listed at the back of this book), and Jupiter, Saturn, Uranus and Pluto all moving into cardinal signs, while Neptune moves into mutable Pisces. The configurations and ingresses during this period bring change on a large scale to every structure in our societies.

This book will explore the Uranus–Pluto squares in the context of the ingresses of the social and outer planets (for instance, Neptune in Pisces and Pluto in Capricorn) and the configurations they make during 2008 and 2015. Examples are given throughout showing how we have arrived at the society we now live in, and what themes will dominate throughout this era. This book is not built on the predictive possibilities that the square may bring but is focused on how, through the lens of the unfolding Uranus–Pluto cycle, our society has grown and reformed.

Much of this book draws on what has taken place in the past in order to understand what is happening in the present day and what we may expect in the future. Through taking a glance at some sectors of society and culture, we will explore the influence of the Uranus–Pluto cycle and the impact of the generation born under the conjunction. A large section of this book is dedicated to the (ironically overlooked) sign of Virgo, the sign in which the Uranus–Pluto conjunction in the 1960s occurred. As we will see, this sign and the traits associated with it are relevant to how our society has been cultivated in the last fifty years.

Sections of this book give snapshot examples of how some of the Uranus–Pluto square challenges have already manifested and been brought to our attention. At the time of writing, the Uranus–Pluto squares have not yet come into exact orb; however, the murmur of the squares has certainly already been felt (in particular, following Pluto's ingress into Capricorn and the cardinal climax of 2010), and the economic recession is an example of this. Other examples of what will be of interest and what may be addressed over the 2012–15 period are highlighted throughout this book.

Uranus and Pluto aspects are often markers of doom and gloom and suggestive of apocalyptic scenarios. This is understandable, as tragedy and uncertainty have prevailed during periods in history when these planets have been in aspect. However, Uranus and Pluto are also exciting energies and they offer new ways and new hope, but a new way of life often only understood or appreciated in hindsight.

It was the best of times, it was the worst of times...
Charles Dickens, *A Tale of Two Cities*

Uranus Meets Pluto

The following section is an introduction to the nature of Uranus and Pluto when they make a hard aspect to each other in the sky. The first section looks at the Uranus–Pluto cycle. As these two planets conjoin in the sky they form a new cycle, a new era is born and this period marks turning points in human history. The more challenging aspects that follow the conjunction of Uranus and Pluto are the square and the opposition, and these aspects coincide with events and changes that are of the nature of the cycle's original conjunction.

The conjunctions, squares and oppositions of previous cycles will demonstrate how the Uranus–Pluto cycle has unfolded in the past – and how each of these challenging times of the cycle shows consistent patterns, describing our social, political and economic landscape.

Understanding how the previous Uranus–Pluto square played out is of huge relevance to us, for we can compare what happened *then* to what is happening *now*. It deepens our understanding of the nature of these two planets and of the meaning and relevance of the cycle. It helps us to grasp the triggers for events such as economic crises, social rebellion and institutional changes, and prepares us for what is around the corner. There are always shocks with Uranus–Pluto – it is the nature of these planets – but understanding their cycle and the previous aspects they have made make it far more interesting from an astrological perspective and probably less alarming from an individual and social viewpoint.

The Uranus–Pluto Cycle

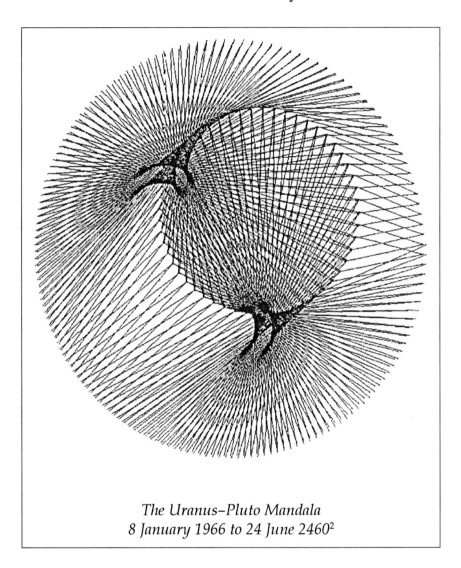

The Uranus–Pluto Mandala
8 January 1966 to 24 June 2460[2]

The cycle of Uranus and Pluto is between 110 and 143 years.
In 1965 and 1966 Uranus and Pluto came into conjunction at
17° and then 16° Virgo – 114 years after their last conjunction.

---

2. Neil Michelson, 'The Uranus–Pluto Mandala: 8 January 1966–24 June 2460',
   Tables of Planetary Phenomena. Michelson perceived this mandala as '... a
   creature with two claws extended, ready to clamp on to an unsuspecting
   victim', p. 227.

The current cycle is 140 years. When these planets conjoined in Virgo in 1965–66, it was the first time in thousands of years they had met in this sign. The last time they conjoined in an Earth sign was in 322 BCE. Prior to their conjunctions in the 1960s, their last conjunction occurred in 1850 and 1851 at 29° and then 28° Aries.

This Uranus–Pluto in Aries period in the mid-nineteenth century heralded a new era of change for human society around the world. It saw pioneering innovations such as planes, steam engines and automobiles which changed history for humankind. Not surprisingly, with a conjunction in the Mars-ruled sign of Aries, we experienced two world wars (one based on the purification of the human race – the pursuit of Aryanism!) This cycle ended with the subsequent conjunction of Uranus and Pluto in the mid-1960s when the planets conjoined in Virgo.

Uranus is associated with the following keywords:

> Eccentric, Unpredictable, Erratic, Shocking, Sudden, Speedy, Idealistic, Utopian, Genius, Reactive, Original, Inventive, Unique, Social, Mental, Detached, Open-Minded, Restless, Impatient, Rebellious, Rule-Breaking, Revolutionary, Independent, Impulsive, Electric, Lightning, Democratic.

On a mundane level, Uranus represents social injustice, rebellion and revolution. It stands for equality and freedom, seeks to liberate oppression, and smashes social norms and 'control systems' that subjugate society. Uranus is unconventional, independent and represents the urge to be free. It is concerned with social ills that permeate society and has a reputation for shaking things up. The planet acts ruthlessly and the nature of its fierceness can be seen in events such as unexpected economic turns, revolts and class rebellion, but can also be seen in mundane planetary events such as earthquakes and lightning storms.

Pluto is associated with the following keywords:

> Power, Survival, Hidden, Secretive, Microscopic,
> Regeneration, Transformation, Destruction, Renewal,
> Death, Birth, Fear, Denial, Sex, Jealousy, Possessive,
> Obsessive, Focus, Control, Primal, Upheaval, Depth,
> the Subconscious, the Underground, Hidden Treasure,
> Finance, Wealth, the Occult, Taboo.

From a mundane perspective, Pluto is represented by that which is dark and hidden within society. This can range from the criminal underworld to mining and excavations, our plumbing and sewage systems, and the social organizations which operate more secretly or more deeply in society. Pluto is considered to be one of the most ruthless of the planets and has a reputation for purging that which is rotten, as it strives mercilessly to get to the root of any matter. Pluto is the planet associated with power; as the Lord of Wealth this planet rules aspects of the economy and also capitalistic forces.

> Come senators, congressmen, Please heed the call
> Don't stand in the doorway, Don't block up the hall
> For he that gets hurt, Will be he who has stalled
> There's a battle outside, And it's ragin'
> It'll soon shake your windows, And rattle your walls
> For the times they are a-changin'.
> Bob Dylan, 'The Times They Are-a Changin'', 1964

When these planets are in conjunction they create social upheaval. They smash and destroy social ills and inequalities and any aspects of society which no longer serve the entire collective. On their own, they are intrepid. Together they are resolute in their intention to radically change the foundation of society in every way – in order to replace it with a new society founded on more egalitarian values.

Uranus and Pluto by conjunction are fearless and far-reaching. Together they dismiss the individual and are interested only in the collective. The beginning of their cycle pinpoints an era when the masses confront in extremity that which they find oppressive. These points in time will show radical and immediate (rather than liberal) action, where power is seized, not negotiated, and where freedom is sought at any cost.

The beginning of the Uranus–Pluto cycle marks a time when people extend beyond themselves for a greater good. Being part of something larger brings anxiety and unrest but also a sense of collective solidarity. A new sense of purpose arises, a new way of seeing and understanding things; a new world view begins to emerge.

Uranus–Pluto is also truth-seeking and demands answers. When these planets come together they mark periods of time where the *existence* and technical workings of every fabric of our being and society become priorities and are deeply explored. These events are highlighted as the planetary cycle unfolds and forms key aspects. Some burning philosophical questions brought by Uranus–Pluto are: what is our place in the universe? What makes us the same and what makes us different? What are we made of? What are our capabilities and how can we evolve? How can we know what we know? When something gets in the way of answering these questions, Uranus–Pluto confronts it and asks, What is stopping us and what can we do about it?

What is our place in the universe?

Here is where we question our relationship to everything else and our position in the larger scheme of things. There is deep understanding of the whole being greater than the sum of its parts, but what is the whole? Under this planetary aspect, there is an urgency to find out what and who is out there that we have yet to be introduced to. This is about understanding the larger environment in which we live. Here, excavating the earth, plunging into the depths of the sea and exploring our space and universe become essential to our comprehension of the relationship between the microcosm and the macrocosm.

We seek to understand our relationship with nature and try to find a way to both assist nature and defend ourselves from its unpredictability.

What makes us the same and what makes us different?

This is about understanding humanity, how we socially interact and what we need to break down so we can become 'one'. Uranus and Pluto together want to smash the boundaries of race, gender and sexual orientation; structures which are divisive and anti-human. The political interface between societies is merely superficial, as is economic disadvantage. While there is focus on human commonality, there is also a need to understand what sets us apart from other species, on and off the planet. Uranus–Pluto seeks to define the truth of our existence and to reveal how we are different (or the same): what sets us apart and what makes humans and other beings alike or distinct.

What are we made of?

At a molecular level we want to understand how our brain functions, how our body works and what our DNA is made up of – how much of this is fixed and how much can be altered or developed. Uranus–Pluto seeks to understand from an engineering perspective where we came from and how we arrived at where we are. Together these planets search for the source of human existence in order to treasure and preserve or eradicate and discard it.

What are our capabilities and how can we evolve?

There is focus here on what we are capable of, from physical strength to the intellectual capabilities of the psychological matrix of the masses. The Uranus–Pluto energy compels us towards progress. It invites us to experiment mentally, physically, socially, economically, politically and sexually to ensure the survival and advancement of the collective. Although it tolerates diversity, it can be indifferent and will seek to make all things the same. It is concerned with the future and how things will be shaped. Based on its own truth it will violently change things for the greater good.

How can we know what we know?

What does the evidence say? Uranus and Pluto work relentlessly to make sure the facts are certain and the truth is just that. Often, however, Uranus and Pluto are creators of their own truth and will devise mechanisms which can count as a double check. Not concerned with the consequences of action, Uranus and Pluto are markers of time where blind-sidedness can develop and where the truth can get a little out of perspective or possibly distorted. The need for change and equality can often be at the very expense of freedom. This is the irony of the nature of these planets. Uranus liberates and Pluto purges but together, as they create crisis and destruction, they can also annihilate. When they break down the existing paradigms and revolutionize culture, there are undeserving casualties along the way.

What is stopping us and what can we do about it?

Uranus and Pluto will endlessly eradicate that which stands in the way of progress and advancement of the masses. The way forward is fundamental, and new paradigms will be developed to create an independent, free-thinking society, where the greater good is of paramount importance. Uranus–Pluto eras dictate a time when all that is perceived to be evil is destroyed, usually violently, so the *correct* order and appropriate human behaviour can be substituted. In order to put things right, one must first establish exactly what has gone wrong.

As the cycle begins, answers to these questions are sought by those living through the conjunction and then are later continuously raised, resolved and implemented by the generation born during it. Issues that arise at the beginning of the cycle unfold and, as the cycle continues, these are spotlighted at every junction throughout the cycle (namely the hard aspects formed throughout it).

There are of course incidents during these periods that are beyond the influence of humanity, such as natural disasters, which remind us of the power and enormity of this cycle. These events remind us of our relationship with nature and our significance (or insignificance) in the larger scheme of Universal life.

The sign of the conjunction is of great importance when analysing the cycle. The sign will colour and shape the areas of life that the cycle is about. For example, when Uranus and Pluto conjoined in Aries, an era of pioneering began, innovative engineering was initiated, men around the world joined the armed forces to fight, and the pursuit of Aryanism began. When the planets came to conjunction in the 1960s in the sign of Virgo, the focus of the cycle was work, health and 'how' to do things. This is discussed at length in the 'Back to the Future' chapter later in this book.

The Uranus–Pluto squares from Aries to Capricorn will occur over the following dates and degree positions:

24 June 2012	8°	Aries and Capricorn
19 September 2012	6°	Aries and Capricorn
20 May 2013	11°	Aries and Capricorn
01 November 2013	9°	Aries and Capricorn
21 April 2014	13°	Aries and Capricorn
15 December 2014	12°	Aries and Capricorn
17 March 2015	15°	Aries and Capricorn

A total of seven exact squares may feel like an ongoing set of aftershocks. Squares in mundane astrology, as Charles Harvey states, are markers of time during which the ideas of the cycle strive to manifest themselves.[3] He goes on to say that the mundane square:

---

3. Charles Harvey, *Mundane Astrology*, p. 199.

represents a striving to manifest, test, and actualize the potential that was inherent in the original conjunction, through a determination to overcome obstacles and meet the challenges of the mundane world... new powers only arise through conscious determination and effort... the developing idea of the cycle will usually be confronted by some kind of crisis which will have to be overcome in order to realize the central ideas and ideals of the cycles...[4]

With any astrological configuration there is a propensity to manifest both positively and negatively. Both manifestations are often found with this cycle and examples will be discussed throughout the book.

---

4. Harvey, *Mundane Astrology*, p. 160.

The Uranus–Pluto Conjunction 1965–66

Uranus and Pluto travelled through Virgo for most of the 1960s: Uranus moved through the sign from 1961 to 1969, and Pluto from 1956 until 1972. While researching for this book, I decided to return to the archives of *The Astrological Journal* to see what was written by astrologers during the 60s about this conjunction.

Julia Parker writes in *The Astrological Journal* in the summer of 1971 about skid kids, 'I often shiver behind my desk while calculating the charts of children born with the Uranus–Pluto conjunction in Virgo. They are on the march already...'[5] Dennis Elwell writes in the Winter issue of 1965/66, 'With Pluto's entry into Virgo ten years ago the cry went up, *Show me how!* – and everything that has met this demand has prospered.' Later in the article he thought that we were entering '*a sort of dehumanization* as one of the dangers of our age. When inspired by forces of Virgo, we focus our attention on the means [but] we are apt to lose sight of the ends. We ought to remind ourselves now and again that where we are going is more important than how we get there.'[6]

Society has changed in that we are primarily concerned with method, technique and how we *do* something, as Elwell warned, rather than being focused on the end result (the destination). This implies that we are more caught up with the Mercurial process and method of 'how' we do something (which very much describes the nature of Virgo), as opposed to the more Jupiterian interest of meaning and 'why' we are doing it. Perhaps there was so little written about this conjunction at the time because Pluto had quite recently been discovered (1930) and wasn't yet so widely used or understood by astrologers.

---

5. Julia Parker, *The Astrological Journal*, Summer 1971, p. 25.
6. Dennis Elwell, *The Astrological Journal*, Winter 1965-66, p. 13.

This era saw unprecedented change on many levels but mostly social and political. The US became involved in the Vietnam War over communism in the early 60s, introducing combat units in 1965, which peaked in 1968. The US withdrew in 1973. During US involvement, anti-war protests were held all over the country.

In 1962, the Cuban Missile Crisis in the Bay of Pigs led to a near nuclear crisis between the US and the Soviet Union, which resulted in the withdrawal of US nuclear weapons from Turkey and the withdrawal of the Soviet Union's nuclear weapons from Cuba. This incident carried the *threat* of global destruction. Together, Uranus and Pluto mark events which plant in the consciousness of society the very real potential and the fear of mass destruction; together they create the image of apocalyptic terror.

The Cold War between the US and the Soviet Union continued, as did the Space Race. Around the world, issues of human rights, democracy, capitalism, communism, social freedom, independence movements and political power struggles were key foci in 1965 and 1966 as the Uranus–Pluto came to exact conjunction.

The young JFK stood for a new era as he attempted to resolve the Vietnam War and Cold War crisis. He was instrumental in the Civil Rights Movement and his assassination was tragic to Americans who dared to believe in a better future.

During the 1960s, while Uranus and Pluto occupied Virgo, several outbreaks of unrest occurred on the political front around the world. Independence from the UK was sought by several African and Caribbean countries. Rwanda became independent from Germany; Algeria sought independence from France and the Nigerian government was overthrown by rebels who killed fifty politicians, including the Prime Minister. Ghana and Guinea had their governments overthrown. The Libyan government was brought down by Gaddafi who announced, 'From this day forward, Libya is a free self-governing republic'.[7] India and Pakistan were at war over Kashmir, and in China the Great Proletarian Cultural Revolution arose, which again was a conflict between capitalism and communism. Over one million people died in this revolution, which had devastating effects on the solidarity of a nation. In Athens, Greece, over 10,000 anti-monarch demonstrators marched against King Constantine. The Berlin Wall was erected and West Germany established friendly alliances with Israel, which saw the breaking of diplomatic relations between West Germany and nine Arab states.

Many of these political movements were led by the generation who had Pluto in Cancer (1912–39). This generation is concerned with protection and strong family ties, which on a mundane level we can understand extends to nationalistic ones. Cancer is about the home, the land, security, and the safeguarding of the boundaries of the home (country) in which we live. Many of this generation had been to war, as their parents had. Cancer is about family and food and Pluto about purging and denial, and this generation endured loss of loved ones and famine on a global scale. The Pluto in Cancer generation understood what it was like to go hungry.

Protests and human rights movements such as the Feminist Movement, the Civil Rights Movement and the Gay Liberation Movement in the West were significant revolutionary forces of this era, as reform was demanded to redress inequalities within society.

This decade is often referred to as the Swinging Sixties: Uranus is about freedom and experimentation and Pluto is associated with sex. The younger generation that drove these changes in this era was the Pluto in Leo generation (1939–58). Leo is also about sexuality, lovers, romance, expression and free love and 'playing around', all of which became fashionable during this period. The summer of love, when

---

7. Nicholas Campion, *The Book of World Horoscopes*, p. 237.

over 100,000 people congregated in San Francisco in 1967 to exert sexual and creative expression, is an example of this. In their youth, the Pluto in Leo generation wanted to party, and Flower Power – the quest for peace and love and mind-altering experiences through experimenting with drugs of all kinds – spearheaded social revolution and challenged ideas of monogamy and women's roles in society, and brought about changes and innovations never before seen in popular culture, music and arts.

Leo rules children and Pluto is about power but also denial. It is not surprising that the empowerment – or the denial – of having children was revolutionized during this period with the introduction of the Pill and the legalization of abortion. As a society, we have yet to recognize to what extent these changes formed the foundations in reproduction technologies and the reconstruction of society and our world views on children, parenthood, population, status and social mobility. More is written on this in the chapter 'Back to The Future – Towards a Virgo Society'.

As the 1960s decade was nearing its end, Uranus entered the air sign of Libra, still within orb of conjoining Pluto, and in the summer of 1969 one of fastest travelling winds ever known, Hurricane Camille, swept through the Atlantic basin; we saw the music festival of Woodstock in the US, where over half a million people attended three days of peace and music; and the first human being set foot on land outside our planet. Neil Armstrong's step onto the Moon proved to be a turning point in human consciousness. Neil Armstrong spoke to over half a billion viewers as he climbed down from the Apollo spaceship: 'That's one small step for a man, one giant leap for mankind'.[8] He was right.

However, another major leap was made earlier in the decade on 23 January 1960, when Jacques Piccard and Don Walsh

---

8. http://www.nasa.gov/mission_pages/apollo/apollo11_40th.html [accessed 4 January 2012].

made the deepest dive (seven miles) into the Ocean at Mariana Trench, just off Guam. No human had ever travelled so deep within the Earth's oceans. Interestingly, this dive will be repeated for the first time since 1960,[9] with a race between film director James Cameron and entrepreneur Richard Branson in March or April 2012. This is interesting given that the first dive of the same magnitude in over fifty years will occur on the Uranus–Pluto square and when Neptune is now in Pisces (the sign linked to the ocean). We shall probably see further ocean dives and discoveries, as well as achievements and advances in space, during this Uranus–Pluto period.

When these giant leaps occur, people's ideologies change. There is nothing quite as exhilarating as discovering the unknown and going where no human has ever gone before! During these times, we start to feel proud of being human, something we do not discuss very often. Uranus–Pluto marks a period of collective identification, an era where we accept that we are all the same. As I write this I am aware that I am the first generation in my lineage to be mixed race – my children are also mixed further. The melting pot society in which many of us now live was spearheaded in the 60s and revolutions such as the Civil Rights Movement in the US made it possible (to some extent) for cultural boundaries to be broken down. In 2008 America voted in its first black President and since the 60s several female Prime Ministers have served to break down existing gender prejudices.

Under the Uranus–Pluto conjunction we sought to understand our place in the Universe, and with that came the desire to explore what else is out there! It is not surprising that the Big Bang Cosmology Theory was confirmed in 1964 (just prior to the Uranus–Pluto conjunction) as the best explanation of the existence of the Universe and life on Earth.[10] Uranus and

---

9. http://deepseachallenge.com/the-expedition/1960-dive [accessed March 2012].
10. Penzias and Wilson, 'A Measurement of Excess Antenna Temperature at 4080 Mc/s', *Astrophysical Journal*, 1965, Vol. 142, p. 419.

Pluto are very much about massive explosions and the theory is very Virgoan in that the bang comes from a single small point in the Universe.

Events and social changes that occurred at the Uranus–Pluto conjunction will be raised again with the seven squares that these planets make between the years 2012 and 2015. Themes, events and 'seed ideas' that occur at the conjunction will be repeated as the cycle unfolds and the planets make challenging aspects to each other. Of course, the organization of the cosmos continues to change, so the setting of the themes (including the signs in which the aspects take place) differ at each point.

Thus, we discover parallels between cyclical points and event points, and these can provide us with not only an understanding of what has gone before but also help us to pinpoint issues that could be raised again in the future. The Uranus–Pluto conjunction of the 1960s had such a huge impact on society and the future of that society, as well as the generations born into it. The aspects that these planets make in transit to each other – such as the current squares and future oppositions, as well as (to a lesser extent) minor aspects, sextiles and trines – will bring attention to these issues once again. The sextile between Uranus and Pluto that occurred in the mid-1990s is an example of this.

For instance, although by the 1960s mankind had already started to view the world as a machine, technological progress since that time has made us see humankind as a machine, too. Reproductive technologies in the mid-1960s set the scene for experimentation on several levels. The first creature to be cloned was a carp in 1963 (when Uranus was approaching a conjunction with Pluto) by embryologist Tong Dizhou in China.[11] Cloning was not publicly debated until the world was told about Dolly the sheep, who caused much

---

11. http://www.pbs.org/bloodlines/timeline/text_timeline.html [accessed Sept 2011].

controversy at the time. Dolly was born on 5 July 1996, when Uranus and Pluto were sextile in our sky.

Another example of parallels between *then* and *now*: on 1 June 1965 there was a terrible accident, when 236 miners were trapped and killed in a mine after a pit explosion in Japan. Recently, as Uranus and Pluto were coming to square and forming a cardinal T-square (with Saturn), a series of similar unfortunate events occurred around the world. In 2009, a methane explosion in a Chinese mine killed 104 people. In August–October 2010, 33 miners were trapped for 69 days in a copper-gold mine close to Chile – to the world's relief they survived! Later that year, in November 2010, 29 men died in a coal mine in Greymouth, New Zealand.

Films, television and music are mediums for entertainment. However, they also include the themes of the era in which they were made and will reflect the cycle that they are in. The production of films for cinema release and pop songs that become hits at a particular period in time give us information as to what is happening on a social level, what people want to see and listen to, and the stories that become popular.

Themes from films and songs from the 1960s (along with all mediums of art) will rise again in our present decade with the current Uranus–Pluto squares. For example, the prequel to the movie *Planet of the Apes* (a 1968 movie that depicts the self-destruction of the human race and puts forward a fictional model of human-ape relationships) was released in 2011, titled *Rise of the Planet of the Apes*. This movie ends with the promise of more of these movies to come, and it will undoubtedly receive attention during the Uranus–Pluto squares. A TV series that aired in 2011 was *The Kennedys*, which told the story of the Bay of Pigs incident in the early 60s. At present, there is talk of a movie about the plight of Martin Luther King in his last years in the mid-60s.

Pop songs and sounds from the 1960s are being re-released by current singers. At the time of writing, two songs at the top of the UK charts are 'Moves Like Jagger'[12] and 'Charlie Brown', all with reference to 1960s phenomena.[13] New songs such as 'Earthquake'[14] have an apt Uranus–Pluto theme. We will undoubtedly see Uranus–Pluto themes or the remake and revival of several 1960s songs throughout the 2010s and we will look at other examples of 60s compositions in this book.

As the Uranus–Pluto conjunction occurred at 16° and 17° Virgo in the 1960s, it is interesting to note when this degree is triggered by transits. For example, when Saturn came to 16°–17° Virgo in September 1979, civil unrest spread as Lord Mountbatten was killed by the IRA, the Pope made the first papal visit to Ireland in the hope of building peace, and the Yorkshire Ripper killed his twelfth victim. The statement released by the police about this warned that 'no woman was safe now'. (Incidentally, 1964 was the worst year for crime in the UK for the entire century.[15]) In 1979, Michael Jackson's *Off the Wall* (quite a suitable Uranus–Pluto and Saturn title) was released and would go on to sell over twenty million copies worldwide. On an even more literal level, the US Pioneer 11 was the first spacecraft to approach Saturn (21,000km away). Saturn returned to the position of 16° Virgo on 7 October 2008 and, along with Pluto's ingress into Capricorn, marked a turning point as the world plunged into economic crisis. On this very day, the meteoroid 2008 TC3 was the first object to have ever been discovered *before* it made impact with the Earth; it exploded in the air above the

---

12. Maroon 5, featuring Christina Aguilera, 'Moves Like Jagger', was released 21 June 2011. The song refers to Mick Jagger, lead singer of the Rolling Stones, which formed in 1962.
13. Coldplay, 'Charlie Brown', was released in the US on 23 January 2012. Charlie Brown is a cartoon character who, although first known in the 1950s through comic strips, had his first television debut in 1965 under Uranus–Pluto.
14. Labrinth, featuring Tinie Tempah, 'Earthquake' released 23 October 2011. Uranus and Pluto by aspect and ingress relate to earthquakes and more is written about this later in the book.
15. http://www.metpolicehistory.co.uk/1946-to-date.html?page=2 [accessed Sept 2011].

desert in Sudan.[16] This of course helps us to identify again our position in the Universe (Uranus–Pluto) and defend (Saturn) ourselves in the future.

---

16. http://news.bbc.co.uk/1/hi/northern_ireland/7964309.stm [accessed Sept 2011].

The Uranus–Pluto Sextile 1995–97

After the conjunction of Uranus and Pluto in Virgo in the 1960s, the next major aspect they made was the sextile between 1995–97. The exact sextiles occurred on the following dates:

10 April 1995	0°	Aquarius and Sagittarius
8 August 1995	27°	Capricorn and Scorpio
8 March 1996	3°	Aquarius and Sagittarius
20 September 1996	0°	Aquarius and Sagittarius
5 February 1997	5°	Aquarius and Sagittarius (with Jupiter at 3° Aqu.)

Themes from the conjunction were brought to our attention during these periods but were different, as the planets resided in different signs and were in a different aspect. In the case of four of the sextiles, the planets were in the signs of Aquarius and Sagittarius, which together are about intellectual endeavours, social freedom and science exploration. Capricorn and Scorpio (the second sextile) are more about social order, sexual matters and that which pertains to birth and death. The sextile is not a challenging aspect like the conjunction, square or opposition and is more about providing opportunity. It represents *a step forward* from the issues raised at the conjunction. A step forward of course may be seen as positive but, in the spirit of Uranus and Pluto, this will still remain controversial.

During this period we saw the birth of Dolly the sheep, as mentioned above, as well as other groundbreaking developments, such as the first woman to be given permission in the UK (on 6 February 1997) to use the sperm of her husband for insemination – two years after his death.[17] In the UK, the abolition of the death penalty for murder came into force on 9 November 1965 and was highly controversial. At the time Uranus–Pluto were partile at 18° Virgo exactly

17. http://www.dianeblood.co.uk [accessed Sept 2011].

opposite Chiron at 18° Pisces, which is widely conjunct Saturn at 10° Virgo. The abolition of the death penalty for all capital crimes in the UK was sealed in 1998. South Africa abolished its death penalty on 6 June 1995 and made provisions for the resentencing of prisoners who had been sentenced to death.[18]

Throughout the 1960s and early 1970s, Angola was in a fourteen-year conflict with Portugal over its independence. As a result of this conflict up to possibly fifteen million landmines were buried within the country during this period.[19] Landmines kill and terrorize (Uranus–Pluto) the people of a country, and Angola has the largest number of land mines of any country in the world. On 15 January 1997, as Uranus and Pluto were coming to their final sextile, Princess Diana spoke out against the landmines and called for a worldwide ban.[20] To date, all countries except the US, Russia and China have signed the treaty banning landmines. During the sextile, Princess Diana also divorced Prince Charles and later had a fatal car accident. Further analysis of Diana is written in the section 'Back to the Future – Towards a Virgo Society'.

---

18. http://www.info.gov.za/view/DownloadFileAction?id=70763 [accessed Sept 2011].
19. http://www.aeaf.org/papers/1997-11-ian-feinhandler.htm [accessed Sept 2011].
20. http://news.bbc.co.uk/onthisday/hi/dates/stories/january/15/newsid_2530000/2530603.stm [accessed Sept 2011].

The Uranus–Pluto Square 1932–1934

As well as revisiting the Uranus–Pluto conjunction of the mid-60s, it is also of value to look at the last time that Uranus squared Pluto (during its previous cycle). This occurred on the following dates:

21 April 1932	20°	Aries and Cancer
02 September 1932	22°	Aries and Cancer
08 March 1933	21°	Aries and Cancer
05 November 1933	24°	Aries and Cancer
18 January 1934	23°	Aries and Cancer

The reason this period is so relevant is because it tells us what we might expect from the upcoming square between these two planets. What is pertinent is that the square in the 1930s was also a cardinal one, from Aries to Cancer, which will have a similar nature to the 2010s cardinal squares that occur in Aries and Capricorn. What makes these two periods different is that the 1930s square was the second (closing) set of squares in a cycle that began with the Uranus–Pluto conjunction in 1850–51.

In the spirit of Uranus and Pluto, the early 1930s saw social, political and economic change; it was not an easy period to live through. The world saw an economic crash (stemming from the stock market crash in the US in October 1929) and high unemployment (fifteen million in the US and six million in Germany), which resulted in hunger in many parts of the world. For a while, banks were closed throughout the US, construction came to a halt and all industry and farming were hit hard. Known as the 'Great Depression', the world went into recession and did not fully recover until after WWII. Again, much of the debate during this period had to do with socialism versus capitalism (or 'industry' as it was seen at the time).

The 1930s also saw the rise of Nazi Germany and fascism. The first Nazi concentration camp (Dachau) opened on 22 March 1933. The next day the Enabling Act of Germany allowed Adolf Hitler to become dictator of the country. In May 1933, the Nazi Party in Germany started book burning and created law to legalize eugenic sterilization, a process administered to those who were deemed imperfect, and a policy devised to create a strong, pure 'Aryan' race. This time was one of the darkest periods that the world had seen for centuries. Over the next few years the world witnessed the genocide of six million human beings and the pain of this is still felt today. Although, historically, the blame has been attributed to Adolf Hitler, what is shocking about this era is that so many other human beings were capable of following the ideology about purifying human beings. It was not just one man but an entire sub-culture that supported this tragedy.

During the early 1930s, conflict was not limited to the US and Europe. For example, the Asian subcontinent had much conflict: there were protests in Thailand against monarch rulership, Japan and China were at war over territorial rights, Hindus and Muslims were in conflict in India, while Gandhi continued to hunger strike for independence, change and to improve life for the people of India.

Uranus and Pluto in hard aspect in the cardinal signs of Aries and Cancer were about strongly defending (Aries) the home front (Cancer). This aspect between these signs has a nationalistic quality and the boundaries of national (Cancer) identity (Aries) became a source of conflict (Aries). Uranus and Pluto are linked to solidarity, but here we see this operating on an exclusive level, which is ultimately divisive. Aries–Cancer conflict is often about *us* and *them* and, given that the conjunction at the beginning of the cycle occurred in Aries, war became a viable course of action at the time. The Uranus–Pluto squares of the 2010s have a similar nature in that they are crisis-orientated. Being cardinal means being armed and motivated. With Pluto in Capricorn (as opposed to Cancer), the squares are not so much about the homeland or the family institution or hunger (although as the opposite shadow sign, these Cancerian matters will be raised) but more about control over the people, the status quo and a clash of perspective as to how society can move forward. During the squares of the 2010s, the fight is not so much about people versus people, but more about people versus authority, and authority versus authority.

As mentioned previously, Uranus and Pluto aspects signify periods when we question who we are, our place on this Earth and within the Universe. Interestingly, the *Planet of the Apes* film, which became a focus during the 1960s and then again in 2011, told a fictional tale of human relationships with our animal brothers and sisters (the Apes). What is so interesting is that during the Uranus–Pluto square in the 1930s, *Tarzan The Ape Man* was released on 25 March 1932, just weeks before the first exact square. March the following year, shortly before the third Uranus–Pluto square, saw the release of the movie *King Kong* (although he was a gorilla). Both films were a huge success. What is fascinating about these movies is that they address a conscious need (and demand) to understand our relationship with those creatures that are most like us on this planet, and perhaps to explore the possibilities of our own evolution.

From this period, two landmark pieces of literature were published that spoke the Uranus–Pluto square loudly. Aldous Huxley's novel *Brave New World* was published on 30 January 1932, twelve weeks before the first square occurred. This book is very much of its era as it addressed the social and economic ills that had been building up at the time. The World State was built on Fordist principles, and mass production and industry became the dominant force in society. In this fictional vision of the future, Huxley wrote about recreational sex and the new forms of reproduction and selective breeding. At the time, it was a controversial book and banned in several countries. Although a work of fiction, it told some interesting truths about the era and predicted some social developments which occurred during later Uranus–Pluto aspects.

The second book that is relevant to the 1930s square is HG Wells' *The Shape of Things to Come*, which was published in September 1933 during the Uranus–Pluto squares. In this work of science fiction, Wells speculates on what will happen in the world up to the year 2106 (interestingly, two years after the next Uranus–Pluto conjunction in Taurus). Many of his predictions have not transpired, but some, such as the use of submarine-launched missiles, became a reality. He predicted the world encyclopaedia would be established in 2012. This is an interesting date given it also represents the exact year of the start of the Uranus–Pluto squares. One could attribute Wikipedia or the Internet or social networks to this vision, or perhaps it has not yet been invented.

The Uranus–Pluto period of the 1930s was a time when people sought freedom from the oppressive regimes under which many of them lived. Interestingly, on 23 May 1934, just after the Uranus–Pluto era ended, Bonnie and Clyde (Bonnie Elizabeth Parker, 1910–34, and Clyde Chestnut Barrow, 1909–34) were shot dead by the authorities. They were outlaws, gangsters and criminal partners in robberies, but were also revered as heroes by several million people during and after this era. What made Bonnie and Clyde so unique is that they challenged the hardship of the 1930s, striking back against economic oppression, and in doing so offered some people hope and liberation from social constraints.

The Uranus–Pluto Landscape of Today

The following section looks at the landscape of the Uranus–Pluto square. In effect, this started with the ingress of Pluto into Capricorn in 2008–09 and Uranus into Aries in 2010–11. It is important to understand these ingresses within a historical context in order to assess what these particular transits are about and what they might bring.

The cardinal crisis of 2010 – when Saturn, Uranus and Pluto made a T-square in the heavens – is also pivotal to comprehending the nature of the Uranus–Pluto square, as it was this astrological configuration that introduced the square. The build-up to it and all that followed have given us some idea of the global crisis experienced by us all. By exploring the economic and geological aspects of this crisis, such as the situation with Iceland, we can see how particular events unfold in predictable, unpredictable and unprecedented ways.

The Ingress of Pluto into Capricorn

The sign of Capricorn represents ambition, social standing and order. On a mundane level, when this sign is transited by Pluto we see anxiety among the population about crime and there is social unrest; the official control of the public's behaviour becomes a priority. Whenever Capricorn is highlighted in the skies, government (and global) agencies introduce new policies and systems of administration to manage the masses. Examples of this include the implementation of tighter border controls, identity cards, the gathering of information about purchasers though store cards, mobile phones, Internet and CCTV, and other 'big brother' technologies. When Capricorn is visited by the outer planets, we see some form of oppression and deprivation, and drastic changes in lifestyles (for better or worse) are noticeable.

Pluto has a need to purge – to clean out the rubbish and discard all that it deems unnecessary. It does the jobs that others are too scared to do, or that are too unpleasant, and has the penetrative skill to get to the bottom of things. Once it has found what needs to be eliminated, it then destroys it. Pluto operates slowly and its effects and transits are around for a long time; it breaks up and annihilates all that is rotten – taking no prisoners.

The devastation left behind brings with it the anticipation of change and renewal and a transformation of power. What existed before no longer remains and must be replaced with fresh, new innovations. As Pluto travels through the zodiac, its sign position tells us the areas that are being transformed irrevocably. When Pluto ingresses into Capricorn, where it was last in 1778, the planet once again visits the sign which is concerned with law and order, economics and the political systems that have become institutionalized into the fabric of society. Every structure that has been put in place since Pluto's last visit is once again under microscopic scrutiny, and those which stand tallest are most vulnerable to change, transformation and 'audit'. When Pluto journeyed into Capricorn in 2008 it was no surprise to astrologers that the world took an economic hit and that we would soon be faced with an unprecedented global recession.

The economic recession that began in 2008 started with the circulation of sub-prime mortgages and resulted in the collapse or bail out of several banks and markets, particularly in the US, the UK and parts of Europe. Stock and property markets started to fall during this period and several people expected the 'cycle' of economic restoration or growth to return. Unfortunately, Pluto is no longer in expansive, speculative Sagittarius but rather in the prudent and ruthless sign of Capricorn, and the economic optimism is not set to return for some time.

Pluto in Capricorn has already seen a fall in the property market throughout the western world, and the demise of financial lenders that support it and the industry (such as estate agencies, retail outlets, building merchants and developers) which is dependent upon it. There has been an incredible downturn in the value of this market and the development of building materials and industry since Pluto's arrival into Capricorn.

The concept of time (and the preservation of it) is associated with Capricorn and its ruler Saturn. As we move into an era of Pluto in Capricorn we are celebrating breakthroughs in technology which will drastically change life expectancy rates. Technological innovations have enabled us to extend life on a scale never seen before in human history. Pluto and Saturn (ruler of Capricorn) are concerned with death but they are also markers of fear. It could be argued that as a society our need to extend life is a reflection of our fear of death (or the unknown).

However, we also find ourselves faced with the global problem of an ageing society, which is reliant on failing welfare systems (particularly in China with its one-child policy); this will continue to be a major concern globally as Pluto makes its slow journey through this sign. As Pluto sextiles (by sign) Neptune in Pisces, issues of how we fare financially and how we provide adequate care for the elderly will be a source of great anxiety. How we value the contributions of the elderly to society will be debated, and certainly a boom in the elderly care and services industry will occur.

The 1976 film *Logan's Run* (based on the novel published in 1967) came to mind while writing this piece. This film was about population control and the (gentle) execution of people when they reached the age of 30 – at their Saturn return! The population was housed inside a dome where all their living requirements were met. The people were not permitted to go outside and were told (falsely) that the air was toxic. This film has a whiff of Pluto in Capricorn sextiling Neptune in Pisces, and this story may be retold in similar ways while Pluto moves through Capricorn.

During this ingress we are challenging the timing of death and this will require the reorganization of social institutions, economic platforms, family relationships and the way we live today.

On the theme of death, there is also a possibility that the way we send our loved ones off or how we would like to be sent off will go through a radical transformation. Funeral services presently can feel like a conveyor belt industry; time slots are rigidly adhered to as one family waits outside the service room and enters immediately after the previous funeral is over. In the UK, funeral costs have also been addressed in the news because they are becoming so expensive that people are unable to afford them! As the funeral industry is put under the spotlight, we will find new and (hopefully) creative ways to make death something that can be accepted more, and find different ways to celebrate someone's life. Technology will play a part here.

When Pluto travels through Capricorn it infiltrates not just the structure of societal systems but the core moral underpinnings on which they were built. It asks, 'Is this right? Are these the correct systems and the appropriate foundations for society – for this particular point in time?' What we know of our own society and where we are placed within it will undoubtedly change before Pluto makes its departure from Capricorn. Each time Pluto travels through Capricorn it changes the worldview of the masses. It shakes up the very bones of society and pinpoints areas related to Capricorn: the skeleton, skin and teeth and how the body functions; clocks, watches and anything to do with measuring time; land and ownership on any scale and the mechanisms through which these are managed; and the domination of industry in all its forms.

With Pluto as its regulator, the transit through Capricorn will also have a huge influence over how society reproduces and populates and how populations can be divided – be it by race, religion, class, etc. Pluto in Capricorn has historically been linked to the development of colonization, science and the economy. No doubt, when Pluto departs from Capricorn there will be evidence of mass destruction and mass regeneration in our society.

We keep hearing that problems of overpopulation are reaching breaking point. The majority of the world's population do not have enough food, while the threat of AIDS and other worldwide epidemics and pandemics increases at alarming rates. As Pluto in Capricorn is the shadow of Pluto in Cancer, food will become a focus once more. With water shortages we will see a reduction in our produce, particularly those that depend so much on water for their growth or production, of which there are many. The scarcity of water will affect farming and agriculture around the globe and new ideas are needed on how this can be managed. The TV show, *The Jetsons* (1962–63), comes to mind, in which the people were so technologically advanced that they only needed to take a pill (with the flavour of their choice) to enjoy and receive all the nutrients they needed. With the mid-60s Uranus–Pluto conjunction occurring in Virgo (Virgo likes little things), plus Neptune in Pisces highlighting water shortages in the present era, this 'pill' idea will probably be revisited.

The Pluto ingress into Capricorn first occurred on 26 January 2008. The following chart is set for London. Two days after the ingress the World Economic Forum Annual Meeting met in Davos, Switzerland. Condoleezza Rice, in her opening address to the meeting, stated the 'the US economy is resilient, its structure sound, and its long-term economic fundamentals are healthy'.[21] At the same forum, Gordon Brown announced that a new type of capitalism was required and that we would need to re-write the Bretton Woods agreement – and he was right. The Bretton Woods agreement was created in July 1944 and from this came the IMF (International Monetary Fund), which is part of the World Bank. It was created to encourage open markets and to maintain currency exchange rates within fixed values. At this forum, Bill Gates addressed the need for creative capitalism and there was much discussion of climate change, food security, water shortages and poverty. Since then, we have seen a complete meltdown of our financial institutions and economic infrastructure. Pluto in Capricorn will bring an end to much of the infrastructure as we know it.

The chart for Pluto's recent first ingress into Capricorn (pictured overleaf) has an applying conjunction to Venus, a wide opposition to Mars and a wide conjunction to Jupiter. Venus rules money and personal worth, Jupiter brings inflation, and with the opposition to Mars we have seen the abrupt changes to our economy in a very short space of time. People's financial worth has been considerably diminished as their homes have been devalued and their pensions shaved. Our inflation rates are high and exchange rates are volatile.

---

21. 'US economy still strong and open: Rice', Reuters, http://www.reuters.com/article/2008/01/23/us-davos-usa-rice-idUSL2388732820080123 [last accessed 27 Sept 2011].

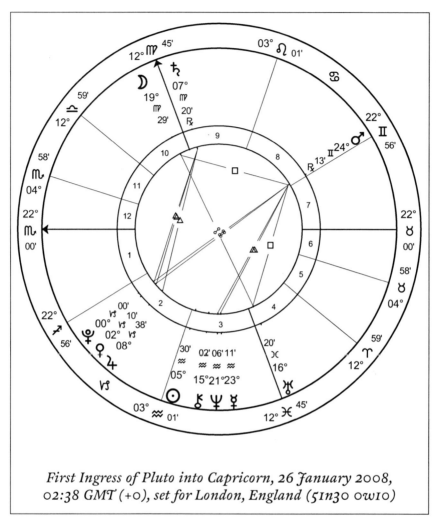

First Ingress of Pluto into Capricorn, 26 January 2008,
02:38 GMT (+0), set for London, England (51n30 0w10)

One occasion when Pluto ingressed into Capricorn with Jupiter was in 1024, not long before England's historically defining moment of 1066. During this period in China there were changes in industry with the development of the spinning wheel (an apparatus which would become one of the most beneficial inventions and biggest assets to mass industry for many centuries), the doubling of the population, and the first paper money was invented!

The only time in the last two thousand years that Pluto made an ingress into Capricorn with a conjunction to Venus was in 1762. Here we saw the introduction of the Industrial

Revolution, with mass industry in the areas of agriculture and the setting up of new financial systems, resource management and new markets, which led to the consumer society that we have today. The ingress conjunction gave rise to a new era in which the focus was on wealth and opportunity. Also at that time, as Pluto was leaving the sign of Sagittarius to enter into Capricorn, we saw the sea explorers transform the maps of the world as new continents were 'discovered' and colonized around the world. The discovery of the New World opened doors for colonial control and the rise of new societies. It will be interesting to watch how the colonization of both space and the oceans will be of focus as Pluto journeys through Capricorn in the current era.

The chart for the second ingress of Pluto into Capricorn in the current era is not as powerful as the first, but it does represent the point where Pluto will remain in Capricorn for the next sixteen years. This chart (pictured overleaf) is set for 27 November 2008 at the location where the Large Hadron Collider was developed (in September 2008). The Large Hadron Collider is the largest of any scientific experiment of our time and is expected to answer questions of physics and the Big Bang Theory, and lead us to a greater understanding about our existence and place in the universe, and the deeper structures of our solar system, as well as the nature of space and time. This chart aptly describes the mammoth event along with the risk involved. There was much discussion at the beginning of the Hadron Collider with regards to the potential creation of micro black holes. These issues were addressed in the media and through the courts but were resolved by several scientific reports saying that there was no 'doomsday' threat.

What is fascinating about this chart is that Pluto not only sits on the IC, the deepest and most underground point of the chart, but it is unaspected, indicating that it is a maverick, explosive and possibly uncontrollable destructive force. However, on a more positive note, it does represent unprecedented change and a search for 'the truth', which

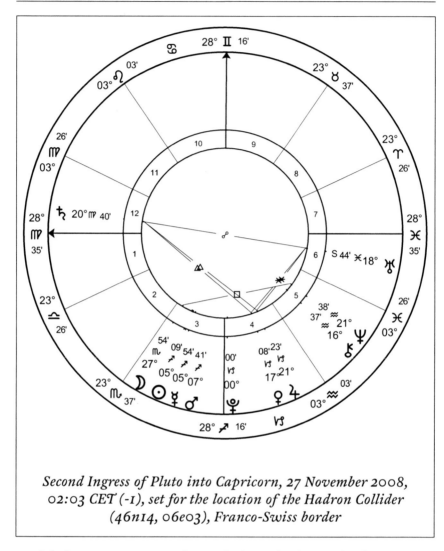

Second Ingress of Pluto into Capricorn, 27 November 2008,
02:03 CET (-1), set for the location of the Hadron Collider
(46n14, 06e03), Franco-Swiss border

could change our entire knowledge of who and what we are
and our place in the much larger scheme of things.

As Pluto digs its way through Capricorn, it is likely that
economic deprivation and depression will increase, and a
sense of anxiety about an unknowable future will permeate
society. Climate change could bring untold problems.
Apocalyptic thoughts will dominate, and fear and anticipation
of prophecies and the end of key periods (such as the Mayan
calendar in 2012) will provide opportunities for this.

It is hard to do justice to the serious nature of the problems outlined here. It is clear that many people around the world have suffered and will suffer the effects of these changes. We can learn from the past and recognize that much that is positive for society has arisen during periods of Pluto in Capricorn, too. We can try to understand what may occur and how people may react in the current climate, and prepare as far as possible to lessen the impact. Astrologers know that with Pluto in Capricorn, resistance is futile, but we need to remain open to new possibilities and opportunities that will lead to the building of social and economic systems.

Pluto requires everything to be 'let go', and it is more painful for those who find it difficult to do so. The cost to humanity and to individuals may be massive in many cases, and seem extremely unfair and difficult to bear, but Pluto is about ruthless necessity, and in hindsight it will be a notable era in the history of our society – one that forces us to change and grow in a new way.

There is anticipation of the squares between Pluto in Capricorn and Uranus in Aries in this period, and out of this inevitable conflict we may see a glimpse of radical new beginnings to come.

As already mentioned, we can gain greater understanding of this square by considering the starting point of the current cycle between Uranus and Pluto. For more on this, see the 'Back to the Future' chapter.

The Ingress of Uranus into Aries

The sign of Aries represents individual choice, freedom and independence, and in mundane astrology this extends from the individual to the collective. When social and outer planets travel through the sign of Aries these issues are highlighted. Separateness and conflict are key areas, as Aries seeks to be self-reliant, challenging and daring. For example, this can manifest in forms of broken alliances or treaties between countries, and nations who wish to become independent from previous associations.

Aries is fiery, impulsive, fresh and naïve; it rarely thinks of the consequences of its actions. When this sign is activated by transiting planets the issue of risk is highlighted, or perhaps the lack thereof. We see examples in the establishment of the Fire Department in Boston, USA, in 1679 when Jupiter, Uranus and Chiron were travelling through Aries. Fire departments of some kind had been around for thousands of years but this particular period saw the introduction of publicly funded fire departments, which set a global precedent; effectively this was about minimizing the risk of fire.

Aries is also related to defence. In mundane astrology we see this represented on a collective scale and military matters are brought into focus. It is no surprise that when NATO was formed on 4 April 1949, the Sun, Mercury, Venus and Mars in Aries (defence) opposed Neptune (the collective); the planets in opposition either trined or sextiled Pluto in Leo.

Each time Uranus moves into Aries it brings the unexpected. Uranus is unpredictable and in Aries it brings an innovative period that heralds new inventions. Pioneering the way for others to follow is a key signature for Uranus in Aries. This configuration is also about collective expression and people will stand up for their rights during this period – it represents protest and the fight for freedom.

Prior to this decade's ingress, the last time Uranus visited Aries was between March 1927 and March 1935, and several innovations and pioneering experiments arose during this period. One in particular which has changed aviation is the iconic transatlantic solo flight made by Charles Lindbergh in 1927. A man nicknamed the 'lone eagle' with Sun and Mars in Aquarius and Moon conjunct Uranus in Sagittarius was the first person to fly between New York and Paris. His successful journey spearheaded several maiden flights across the oceans. A year later, Amelia Earhart was the first woman to fly as a passenger (later as a pilot) across the Atlantic.

Other advancements indicative of Uranus in Aries in this period were the discovery of DNA, the introduction of airmail, the first air-conditioned office (San Antonio), the first balloon flight over 40,000 feet (Illinois), the first transatlantic telephone call, the invention of radio and film and the opening of the Cyclone Rollercoaster on Coney Island, USA. Aries is about speed and pioneering and Uranus brings attention to that which is lifted off the earth (into 'space'), matters of intellect and is future orientated. Together they are exciting and invigorating and the period (1927–35) revealed innovation in electronics, mathematics, physics and quantum mechanics. Uranus in Aries is the brave and unbreakable man and it is no surprise that Superman, the superhero who could jump buildings with a single bound, was created in 1932 during Uranus's last visit to Aries.

The ingress of Uranus into Aries saw the overturn of the roaring twenties and mass consumerism, and (along with other astrological contributing factors) saw the Wall Street crash of 1929, which was the start of the Great Depression. This was also a time where people were rising up in protest: in the US, there was the women's suffrage movement and fight for voting and full citizenship.

The energy of Uranus works well in Aries, and with this placement there is a sense of urgency, a need to stir things up, as if a surge of adrenalin is running through society, which is perhaps evident by the rebellions in the Middle Eastern countries since it entered the sign.

This placement is not always easy. Uranus in Aries can be unpredictable, shocking and likes to shake things up, and events such as earthquakes and cyclones are some possible manifestations. In August of 1927, the Nova Scotia Hurricane, which took 184 lives, was an example of this. On 7 March 1927, as Uranus entered Aries and then went retrograde back to 29° Pisces, an earthquake hit Japan killing almost 3,000 people. The Japan earthquake of 11 March 2011 also took place when Uranus had recently entered Aries and then had gone retrograde to 29° Pisces. The latter earthquake we know to be the cause of the tsunami (Pisces) which then devastated the country. Often planets at their final degree of a sign have a sense of urgency and there are frequently significant events which depict the nature of the planet as it exits the sign.

Uranus made its first ingress (in recent history) into Aries on 28 May 2010. That day, Jonathan Trappe floated over the English Channel on a chair attached to a cluster of 54 helium balloons and was reported in the *Daily Mail* on 29 May.[22] On the same day, *The Daily Telegraph* reported how parachutist Jonathan Tagle surfed on the back of a skydiver (Jeff Nebelkopf) over Moab, Utah.[23] These are two of the more positive examples of the ingress of Uranus (conjunct Jupiter) in Aries.

What makes the 2010 ingress of Uranus into Aries different from other periods in time is that not only is it conjunct Jupiter but it is also square Pluto and opposite Saturn. It was building towards the cardinal T–square later that year, which has since played out through the financial crisis around the globe. The Uranus in Aries part of this T–square brings the

---

22. http://www.dailymail.co.uk/news/article-1282096/Adventurer-Jonathan-Trappe-crosses-Channel-chair-tied-helium-balloons.html [acc. 29 May 2010}
23. http://www.telegraph.co.uk/news/picturegalleries/theweekinpictures/7779507/The-week-in-pictures-28-May-2010.html?image=2 [accessed 28 May 2010].

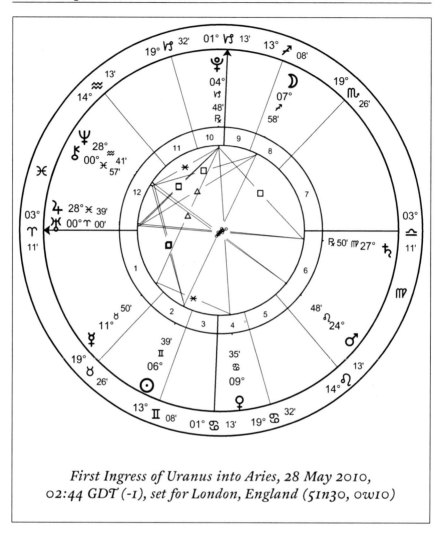

First Ingress of Uranus into Aries, 28 May 2010,
02:44 GDT (-1), set for London, England (51n30, 0w10)

element of unpredictability. It creates a mass uncertainty of
what is to come. It also has a savvy quality about it, where
survival (emphasized by Pluto) and 'getting on with it' (Aries)
becomes an integral part of how people deal with the crisis.
People start to expect the unexpected; they become immune
to shock and start adjusting their lifestyles to make the best of
the situation. Uranus in Aries is fearless, which counteracts
the qualities of Pluto in Capricorn and Saturn in Libra, both
of which are concerned with conservatism and preserving
the status quo. Uranus in Aries wants to break this down; it
is not interested in materialism but rather a *fair* way of living,

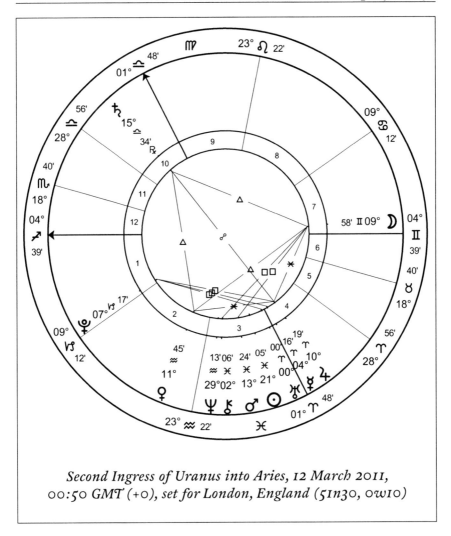

Second Ingress of Uranus into Aries, 12 March 2011,
00:50 GMT (+0), set for London, England (51n30, 0w10)

and it tends to take on a 'nothing to lose' quality, which is evident in the Middle Eastern rebellions and the western world's protests and riots.

The second ingress of Uranus in Aries (chart above) occurred on 12 March 2011 and the planet will remain in Aries until 2018, when it makes its entry into Taurus.

The second ingress of Uranus is accompanied by Mercury and both are square to Pluto. Mercury in mundane astrology, along with the third house, represents the media. Set for

London, Pluto resides in the first house, Uranus in the third house and Mercury in the fourth house (in the Placidus house system). There are other aspects at play here too, but if we isolate this square we can see the difficult dynamics of the shocking (Uranus) exposure (Pluto and first house) of and through media (Mercury and third house) which brings the abuse of authority (Capricorn) into question.

In between these two ingresses, we saw the arrest of Julian Assange, founder and Editor-in-Chief of WikiLeaks, in relation to a sexual crime (Pluto) in Sweden. This was announced around the same time as the WikiLeaks site began to whistle-blow confidential documents of governmental communications from all over the world – including 251,000 US diplomatic cables – in the name of freedom of expression, and reignited the debate about censorship and the freedom of the press. Assange's WikiLeak revolution has been attributed with triggering the rebellion in Tunisia, as it exposed the corruption of the President's family and leadership.[24] It is fitting that Mercury is in the fourth house, as Assange (symbolizing Mercury) was granted temporary asylum in England, although being conjunct Uranus and square Pluto, he was electronically tagged and granted conditional bail.

As is common with astrological configurations, we see a variety of manifestations of a similar nature. On the same theme of media exposure, four months after the Uranus ingress, *The News of the World* publication was forced to shut down (10 July 2011) after 168 years in operation, as reporters of the publication were investigated and exposed for phone-hacking the families of missing persons, victims of crime and soldiers who died in action, plus celebrities and royalty. Rupert Murdoch, one of the richest and most influential men of our time, was the head of the newspaper group and was investigated for corruption and bribery in the UK and the US.

---

24. See http://wikileaks.foreignpolicy.com/posts/2011/01/13/wikileaks_
and_the_tunisia_protests and http://www.businessinsider.com/tunisia-
wikileaks-2011-1 [accessed 31 March 2012].

Interestingly, Murdoch was born on 11 March 1931 under a Saturn, Uranus and Pluto T-square. The then Editor-in-Chief Rebekah Brooks was arrested on 17 July 2011 in connection with the phone-hacking allegations. She was born on 27 May 1968, under the Uranus–Pluto conjunction.

As much as Uranus–Pluto is attributed to the technological revolution spearheaded in the 1960s, the other side to this is 'hacking' – digging into areas electronically where no one else dares to go, and as Uranus and Mercury entered Aries in 2011, we witnessed the shocking exposure of the media in many forms; and with the exact squares, we can probably expect a lot more of this to come.

The Cardinal Climax

A cardinal climax[25] occurs when the outer planets make hard aspects to each other in the cardinal signs. This occurs approximately every 80–90 years and the last time we saw this was in the early 1930s with the Great Depression. With a cardinal climax there tends to be an economic crisis and the climate of the time results in populations feeling anxiety, dread and fear. Until it comes to an end, it can feel like the light at the end of the tunnel is nowhere to be found.

Before 2008, when Pluto entered Capricorn, if anyone had been told that their money might not be safe in a bank they would never have believed it. Although this information is a little out of date it does illustrate the perspectives and foresight of the economy at the time. The end of the Pluto in Sagittarius era made the world aware of the unprecedented debt (on both a personal and national level) that had spiralled out of control throughout the previous decade.

In 2007, just prior to the ingress of Pluto into Capricorn, we saw the fall of Northern Rock (a very Capricorn name) and the introduction of the credit crunch (again, Capricornian in nature). It highlighted the importance of cutting costs and expenditure and the desperate need to pull in the reins. By 2008, the economic system from the Pluto in Sagittarius period of increased spending and escalating debt no longer worked. No matter how long people wait for things to get back to 'normal', the goalposts have now permanently shifted. (Pluto won't return to Sagittarius for another two and a half centuries.)

In August 2010, Uranus and Jupiter at 0° and 2–3° Aries respectively opposed Saturn at 1° Libra and both squared Pluto at 3° Capricorn, forming a cardinal T-square, the so-called 'cardinal climax'. Many astrologers expected drastic,

---

25. This phrase was coined by astrologer Ray Merriman in 1994.

global events around that date, but these planets started to make their mark before and continued to influence well after the exact aspect. Orbs for the outer planets can be wide, for example when Pluto makes a conjunction to our Sun or Moon we will feel it long before the conjunction is exact and for a long time after. It does not always depict a precise event but rather a life-changing experience across an era. We know once it has passed that things will never be the same again and this feeling is now being shared around the globe. The cardinal climax is still being felt and the world is in economic and political turmoil, which can be expected to continue until some time after the seven Uranus–Pluto squares between Aries and Capricorn have been completed.

Currently in the UK, we are living in a society where people are not buying property and many home-owners are in negative equity. First-time buyers often cannot raise the deposit needed for their purchase and, even if they can, it is challenging to get a mortgage. Banks are either not lending or have tightened their criteria. We become hopeful when public spending increases by a percentage or when property sales increase by a fraction, but as our VAT, taxation, fuel and utility costs also increase, so does our credit card expenditure, unemployment rates and inflation. Britain is not alone in this financial predicament.

Since July 2011, Greece had been under the spotlight as it desperately needed to get its first austerity package approved before it received a bail-out of 12 billion euros, which is only part of the 110 billion euros it will receive from the International Monetary Fund (IMF) over the years. This particular country has created much anxiety for Europe and the rest of the world because if Greece had not been bailed out it would have defaulted on its sovereign loans and could effectively go bankrupt. One needs to ask how this could affect the entire European economy, not just with the instability of the euro but also with the stakeholders of Greek debt. How would Germany fare, given that they are Greece's largest creditor? France is also a major creditor for Greek loans and we have learnt that China has bought much of Greece's debt. The bail-out resolves a short-term problem but is only a Band-Aid in terms of healing this dilemma, as Greece's debt at the beginning of 2012 amounted to 160 per cent of its national output. How can any country manage such a financial burden, particularly with a 16 per cent unemployment rate that is rising? Many Greek people have been infuriated by the approval of the bail-out, and violent protests and riots are raging because many Greeks understand that the conditions imposed by the austerity package may not be in their best interests and that they will ultimately pay for the bail-out.

Greece is not the first country, and nor will it be the last, to be hit by the economic crisis. Ireland and Portugal have already been affected and Spain and Italy are in similar difficulties. France and Germany appear to remain strong but they too are vulnerable when other European countries are suffering. Any European country that is challenged economically or politically in this climate will have a dire effect on the stability of the euro as well as on the countries and institutions that have loaned money to the country. We have been informed that China has been told not to buy any further US debt and has bought much of the European debt, although to date we do not know exactly whose or how much!

So what can astrology tell us about what is going on at present? We have Europe and the US in an economic crisis and major political upheaval in North Africa and the Middle Eastern countries. Many techniques can be used to look at these problems but a country's national chart can provide some insight into what and why these crises are occurring.

Here is a reminder of when the Uranus–Pluto square from Aries to Capricorn will be exact from 2012–15 on the following dates and degree positions.

24 June 2012	8°	Aries and Capricorn
19 September 2012	6°	Aries and Capricorn
20 May 2013	11°	Aries and Capricorn

01 November 2013	9°	Aries and Capricorn
21 April 2014	13°	Aries and Capricorn
15 December 2014	12°	Aries and Capricorn
17 March 2015	15°	Aries and Capricorn

Another interesting time will be April–May 2014 when Jupiter will also join the square, creating a T-square to Uranus and Pluto from its position at 11°–15° Cancer.

The national charts with planets and angles at early degrees of the cardinal signs (from 0°–10° degrees) will be triggered by the cardinal T-square of 2010 and some of the seven squares that will occur between Uranus and Pluto. We can expect to see crisis, conflict and challenge to those countries. As the square progresses through the signs of Aries and Capricorn we will see the planets that occupy later degrees of the cardinal signs of national charts being activated. The partial solar eclipse at 9° Cancer on 1 July 2011 will also have some bearing on the political leaders and status of these countries.

The Uranus–Pluto square, like its conjunction in the 1960s, brings about protest and revolution connected with civil and human rights. During the 1960s when Uranus and Pluto came together by conjunction, there were riots that demanded equality and raised concern for humanity. Issues of democracy as well as women's rights were also addressed, and the first square between these planets is now bringing these issues into the spotlight once again.

Pluto in Capricorn square Uranus in Aries is about breaking down the status quo and the existing structures that no longer serve a society. Uranus in Aries is about asserting freedom, individual and collective choice, and when it is square to Pluto in Capricorn it will bring head-to-head conflict with the institutions and governments that support the 'old way'. There is need for change, and any change is born out of crisis and will perhaps be strongly indicated in the national chart.

It is important to note that astrologers can use different charts for a particular country. However, each of these charts represents a major change in the political or economic structuring of that society. When there are several charts, or a hierarchy of charts, for a particular country, these can also be seen as transits to the original chart that we have. For example, the UK 1801 chart shows Pluto at 2°42' Pisces – as does the 1066 chart. Thus, we can see that the 1801 chart depicts a Pluto return for the 1066 period.

Here is a brief look at the range of Northern African charts for countries who have already, or are currently, experiencing political disorder and unrest. It is interesting to see how many possess planets or angles at early cardinal points and which are being triggered by the Uranus–Pluto square:

Tunisia 1956	Venus	4° Cancer
Libya Independence 1951	Sun	1° Capricorn
	Chiron	4° Capricorn
	Jupiter	5° Aries
Libya Republic 1969	Uranus	2° Libra
	Chiron	5° Aries
	Mercury	7° Libra
	Jupiter	8° Libra
Egypt Independence 1922	Venus	1° Aries
	MC	4° Libra
	Saturn	5° Libra
	Pluto	7° Cancer
Syria 1944	Neptune	4° Libra
	Sun	9° Capricorn

If we look at the economic crisis and those countries that have suffered so far, we find the following:

Ireland 1916	Pluto	1° Cancer
Ireland 1948	Mercury	4° Capricorn
	Jupiter	7° Capricorn
Portugal Revolution 1910	Mars	8° Libra
	Sun	10° Libra
Portugal Democratic	Saturn	0° Cancer
Regime 1974	Mars	3° Cancer
	Pluto	4° Libra
Greece Revolution 1821	Chiron	2° Capricorn
	Neptune	3° Capricorn
	Uranus	3° Capricorn
	Sun	4° Aries
	Mercury	4° Aries
	Jupiter	5° Aries
Greece Independence 1822	Moon	2° Libra
	Neptune	3° Capricorn
	Uranus	4° Capricorn
Greece Kingdom 1830	Pluto	6° Aries
	Jupiter	6° Capricorn
Greece Democracy 1974	Venus	3° Cancer
	Pluto	4° Libra
	Moon	4° Libra
	Mercury	10° Cancer

Other vulnerable charts that may need to be taken into consideration are as follows:

IMF	Sun	5° Capricorn
	Neptune	8° Libra
Euro currency beginning	Asc	2° Libra
	MC	3° Cancer
	Sun	10°
Capricorn		
Euro currency circulated	Asc	0° Libra
	MC	0° Cancer
	Chiron	2° Capricorn
	Venus	7° Capricorn
	Sun	10°
Capricorn		
	Jupiter	10° Cancer

In addition to these, our own UK charts show sensitivity to cardinal points:

UK Coronation 1066	Sun	9° Capricorn
UK Union 1801	Uranus	1° Libra
	Asc	7° Libra
	MC	9° Cancer
	Sun	10° Capricorn

The 1801 chart (see overleaf) is the most commonly used chart for the UK and we can see that not only will the angles be triggered by the Uranus–Pluto squares but the Sun will, too. In the late 1980s, when Saturn, Uranus and Neptune came to conjunct the IC and Sun of the 1801 chart, astrologer Charles Harvey predicted a major property market crash (as Capricorn sits on the fourth house cusp, and both Capricorn

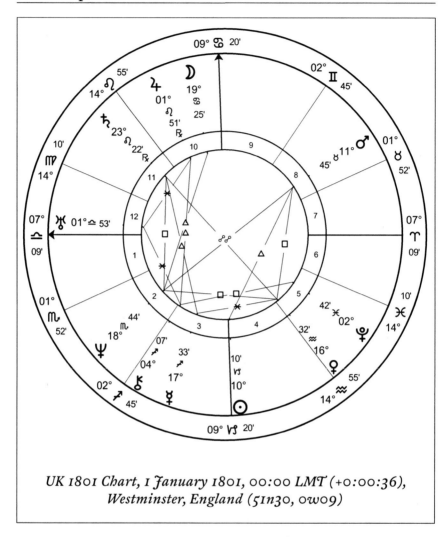

UK 1801 Chart, 1 January 1801, 00:00 LMT (+0:00:36),
Westminster, England (51n30, 0w09)

and the fourth house are associated with property).[26] He sold
his house and rented instead in anticipation of the crash – he
was right!

The first transit of Uranus–Pluto falls in the third and sixth
houses of the 1801 chart. Here we have third house issues such
as schools and education, railways, the postal system and
libraries, and sixth house issues of work and health coming
under the spotlight. There is already talk by the current

26. Conversations with friends and colleagues of Charles Harvey.

government[27] to expand grammar schools and overhaul the current transportation system. In the current climate we are also witnessing libraries shutting down and post offices now reliant on advertising for survival. Although now disbanded, the Greater London Council (GLC, which was formed exactly on the Uranus–Pluto conjunction in 1965) was responsible for moving forward the creation of the M25 (the orbital motorway surrounding London), and will also undoubtedly receive attention during the squares. Sixth house issues of the moment include the increase in unemployment rates and problems with welfare services, such as the National Health Service (NHS), that are not up to standard.

As the first square becomes exact, Uranus will conjunct the UK's Descendant (opposing the Ascendant), and Pluto will square them, creating a T-square whose apex is in the third house of the UK chart. The third house is also about neighbours and here we may see debates and major changes to what constitutes the United Kingdom or Great Britain. There are already more serious talks about Scotland becoming a separate country, and this may very well happen – it may not be alone in gaining independence from the UK either. Wales and Northern Ireland may also move in this direction, as the third house remains afflicted by this transit. Uranus in Aries on the Descendant could bring about the breaking of treaties and relationships with previous allies (as well as possibly forming new ones with unexpected partners). We have already seen this occurring with David Cameron not supporting European leaders on their financial rescue. While the UK has a coalition government, its stability may become vulnerable during this period.

With Uranus in Aries opposing the Ascendant, and Pluto squaring Uranus and the Ascendant–Descendant axis and then later conjoining UK Sun, there may be some radical shift of both the image and identity of the UK and we may live

---

27. At the time of writing, the UK government is a Conservative-Liberal
    Democrat Party coalition, with David Cameron as Prime Minister.

through a time where the UK is renamed or repositions itself in the global scheme of things. Interestingly, when the Uranus–Pluto conjunction occurred in the 1960s, several countries became independent from British colonization. With the square, we can expect to see similar calls for independence. As the square builds, Neptune and Chiron travel over Pluto in the UK chart. With Pluto also as co-ruler of the second house, the UK may find itself dissolving the financial institutions that have governed the country for long periods of time. As the square travels into the fourth and seventh houses of the UK chart, again this can indicate that our property market and the industries that survive on the market will become at risk, as will farming and agriculture of the land. Long-term relationships held within the country and with those outside may become unhinged. There is opportunity here to rebuild both the land and relationships, and this period may see a new dawn for the UK.

One country that has been afflicted majorly by the cardinal crisis is the US. Opposite is the Sibly chart for the US. In this chart, Uranus and Pluto make their first square between the first and fourth houses, both cardinal houses (similar to the UK chart). The square also makes a T-square with the Sibly chart's Venus, Sun and Jupiter, which reside in Cancer in the seventh house, and later form a Grand Cross with Saturn in Libra in the tenth house.

The first house is associated with the identity of a country and the image it projects to the rest of the world. With Pluto travelling through the first house it will bring change to this image. The US was considered 'the' superpower and this has begun to change since Pluto's ingress into Capricorn in 2008 and the cardinal climax in 2010. The US lost its triple-A credit rating in 2011 for the first time ever.[28] With the square occurring to the fourth house there is some concern over the people who need to be looked after in the US. So many of

28. http://www.bbc.co.uk/news/world-us-canada-14428930 [accessed 28 Nov 2011].

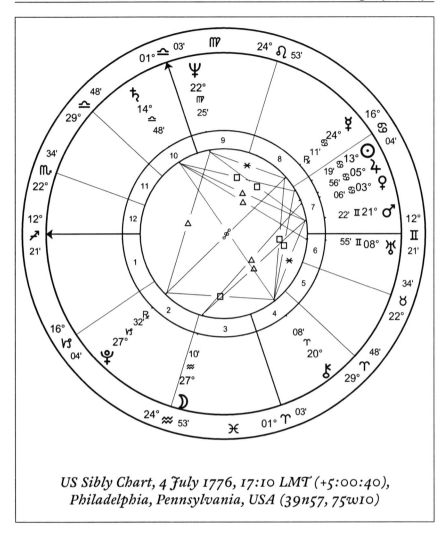

US Sibly Chart, 4 July 1776, 17:10 LMT (+5:00:40),
Philadelphia, Pennsylvania, USA (39n57, 75w10)

this great nation's people have lost their homes and, with the fourth house afflicted by the first house, issues of home, food and family will be highlighted here. This configuration in the US chart is a battle to save the past and fight for the homeland, and represents the land and native roots and historical matters that may come to light which need addressing during the Uranus–Pluto squares. Uranus in Aries in the fourth house square Pluto in Capricorn in the first will also bring to attention matters of populations and borders and we may witness changes in Green Card and immigration policy, particularly as the planets in the Sibly chart's seventh house are triggered here, too. Exactly what it means to be an American will be revised. Land issues and property rights could become a rising conflict during the period of the Uranus–Pluto squares.

Venus is the first planet in the Sibly chart to be triggered by the squares, and as the dispositor of the sixth and tenth houses we see challenges arising with work (specifically rising unemployment rates) as well as career aspirations and opportunities for the American people.

A particularly vulnerable time for this chart is 21 April 2014 when the fifth exact square of Uranus–Pluto makes a T-square to the Sibly Sun and creates a Grand Cross with only a one degree orb to Saturn in Libra in the tenth house. This will be a time when the US will become accountable as never before and when the President in particular comes under the radar. These are cardinal signs in cardinal houses and crisis will elevate during this period and bring up issues that were first addressed during the economic crisis, starting with the collapse of Lehman Brothers in 2008. This will be a difficult time for the US and long-held alliances will no doubt be needed.

Two countries which have come under the spotlight in recent years are India and China. There is much speculation that these two countries, with such huge populations and technological advances, will become the next global superpowers.

India's chart (opposite page) is set for the Indian Republic date and time and has cardinal angles with an Aries Ascendant and Capricorn Midheaven. These angles will pick up the cardinal climax and tension will be felt in the areas related to the first and tenth houses. Besides Uranus in Cancer, there are no other cardinally placed planets. There may be some pressure on the technological movements of this country during the time of the squares and, with Cancer on the fourth house cusp, issues with neighbouring country Pakistan and there may be some change in the outsourcing facilities that India offers to other countries such as the UK. However, with transiting

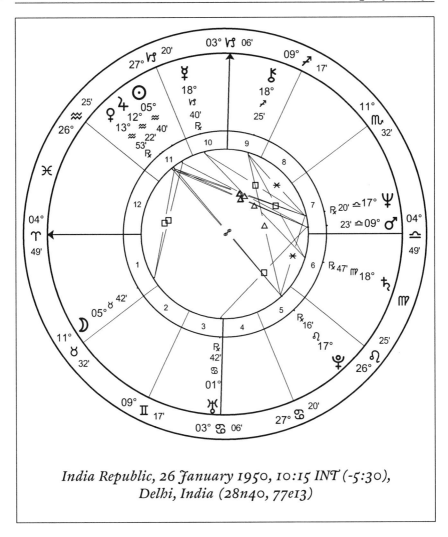

India Republic, 26 January 1950, 10:15 INT (-5:30),
Delhi, India (28n40, 77e13)

Neptune trine Uranus, and as Jupiter travels through Taurus and India's second house, there is some relief here. India can probably relax for a few years and start collecting resources for the new tomorrow during the Uranus–Pluto squares.

When outer planets transit the angles, the areas triggered are not nearly as complex as when they aspect a planet in the chart. The transits of these planets to the Ascendant and Midheaven to India's chart could indicate, as in the UK and US charts, some change in identity. The world may see India repositioned and through a different light and, conversely,

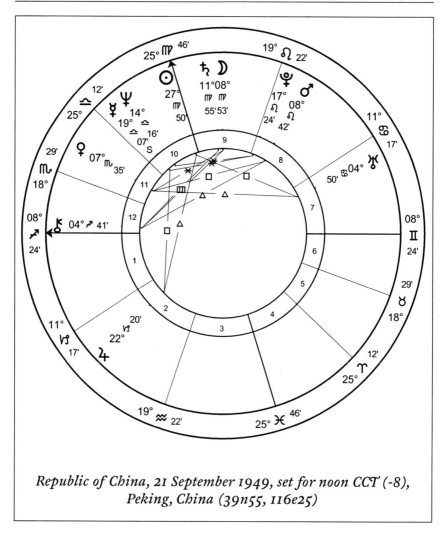

Republic of China, 21 September 1949, set for noon CCT (-8),
Peking, China (39n55, 116e25)

the population of India may change their views towards their allies and foes and see the world in quite a different way.

China's chart is set for the People's Republic of China. Similar to the US chart, China has Sagittarius rising, which always gives a hopeful and optimistic image to the world, although with Chiron close to it (from the twelfth house) there may be some dread or paranoia which may be the motivating force behind the growth of China. China has four planets in cardinal signs – Uranus is at 4° Cancer, Neptune at 14° Libra, and Mercury at 19° Libra, which makes a square to Jupiter at 22° Capricorn.

The cardinal climax will bring in China as a major player on the global playing field. Uranus is the first planet to be triggered by the Uranus–Pluto squares and in Libra and in the seventh house we see similar themes in the previous countries' charts which bring up issues of relationships with others. Uranus is also the co-ruler of the third house so here there may be some tension with neighbouring countries and communication systems within the nation. Uranus is also disposited by the Moon (which rules the people) and is conjunct Saturn (which rules deprivation) and both reside in the ninth house. This may bring rise to an imbalance of economic resources and raise issues of equality.

From April 2014 through to March 2015, Uranus in Aries squares Pluto at 13°, 12° and then 15° Capricorn. These transits will also pick up Neptune in Libra in the tenth house, perhaps dispelling certain myths people have about China. These later squares occur in the second and fourth houses of the country's chart, and we will see some tension with the financial and property markets in the region. There will be discussion about letting go of ownership of debt and assets as people may question whether territories *belong* to China, or it may be that China takes possession of new regions – and it could be in a legal and financial position to do so. Defaults on loans result in repossession and in our lifetime we might see such radical methods used between nations.

Of course, when looking at a country's chart, other factors need to be taken into consideration here, such as the aspects within each of the charts and the rest of the planetary positions. We can see inconsistencies in which of the cardinally placed planets are triggered. There are also many other countries with planets or angles at early cardinal degrees which may not have been affected so directly. These charts each need further analysis in order to understand exactly what is going on, but this is more of a brief summary and general commentary on early cardinal points in these particular national charts.

The economic crisis is not confined to a specific bank, single country or any particular continent – it is a global problem. Band-Aiding any single currency, or temporarily fixing an economic or political crisis in isolation, does not address the major issue with which the cardinal climax and the Uranus–Pluto square are concerned. This is about breaking free (Uranus) from the old and creating something new (Aries). It is about letting go (Pluto) so change can take place and new structures (Capricorn) that will serve society can be formed. The current debt around the globe, at both a personal and national level, requires restructuring and new systems are needed to function so they may cater for an ever-changing society. This is not an easy time but, as astrologers, we understand that something new will come from this. It is not all doom and gloom but more about weathering the crisis and contributing to its development in a way that works economically and in the best interests of the people. In hindsight, this period will undoubtedly indicate a positive major shift in the consciousness of society.

The Meltdown and Firing Up of Iceland

Iceland is a country with a population of approximately 300,000 people and throughout the late 20th century it profited from two main industries: fishing and the production of power and aluminium (it is a country rich in glacial rivers and geothermal heat). Iceland is unique in the way it regulates its national fishing industry. In the 1970s, Iceland won the 'cod war' against Britain, which resulted in Britain's expulsion from Icelandic waters.[29] Soon after, the government of Iceland basically privatized fishing, in that fishermen were allowed by law to catch a certain quota of fish per annum. How much fish could be caught was decided by the historical catches of each fisherman. This quantity was fixed and enabled fisherman to sell their guaranteed quota on to other fishermen if they chose to do so. Fishermen were even allowed to borrow against their annual quota and banks had no problem assigning a dollar value to a particular volume of cod pulled – without competition. Being able to privatize fish and then borrow against it, however, led to the securitizing of this commodity.[30] This innovative manner of doing business would soon be applied to a new industry – investment banking! An industry which would see Iceland's economy enjoy an unparalleled boom in the first decade of the 21st century, and suffer a subsequent and inevitable meltdown in 2008.

Iceland is unique as a nation. Although the population is small, it is highly educated; young people are encouraged to study abroad, they are hard-working, seldom idle and share one religion (Lutheran). There are only nine surnames used within the nation. The banks were state-owned until 2002 when the government privatized them as well as lowering taxes, privatizing industry and freeing up trade.[31] The result

---

29. Asgeir Jonsson, *Why Iceland?* p. 37.
30. Michael Lewis, *Boomerang*, pp. 29-30.
31. Lewis, *Boomerang*, p. 15.

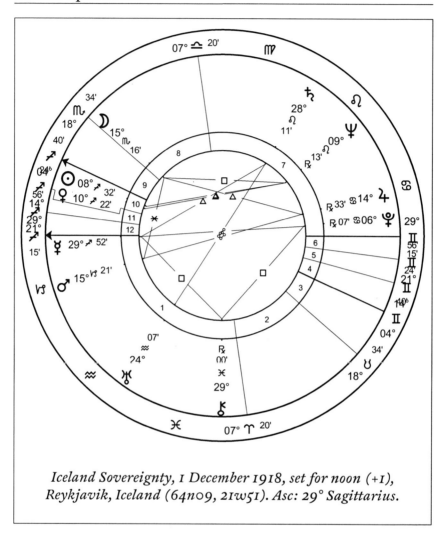

*Iceland Sovereignty, 1 December 1918, set for noon (+1),
Reykjavik, Iceland (64n09, 21w51). Asc: 29° Sagittarius.*

of this was that Iceland became the fastest growing economy
on the planet and several Icelanders left their fishing boats
and entered the investment banking industry. As a small
nation, there was little interest from other countries to invest
in Iceland (except for a small amount in aluminium smelting)
but due to the size of the country it was easier to transfer
capital and play with the markets as there were fewer
bureaucratic intermediaries or formal financial regulators.
Everyone in the business pretty much knew everyone else
– they were a community of bankers who shared an 1100-
year history. Due to the nation's long-term exemplary credit

rating, Iceland became an excellent international customer to lend to. Icelanders very quickly learnt the art of investment banking and in a very short space of time Iceland proved to be one of the fastest and largest rising economies in the world – although this was to be short-lived.

Bankers started to play with the exchange markets, borrowing from one currency and spending on another. For example, when their own interest rates were at 15.5 per cent they borrowed the Yen at 3 per cent to buy what they would not normally have been able to afford.[32] Icelandic bankers started buying assets abroad with money that had been borrowed – assets the value of which they thought could only rise. The bets they hedged were mostly on foreign markets funded by foreign banks. In 2003, the asset base of the banks of Iceland was worth a few billion dollars. However, over the next three and a half years, this grew to over $140 billion. It was the most rapid expansion of any banking system in the history of mankind. While the value of the US stock market doubled during this period, Iceland's stock market value multiplied nine times.[33]

Nick Campion documents two charts for Iceland. The first (opposite) is set for 1 December 1918 when Iceland, after more than 500 years, was granted legal sovereign independence from Denmark (although the Danish king remained head of state).[34] This chart aptly describes the adventurous nation after it became independent: a chart with three planets in Sagittarius (Sun, Venus and Mercury) where Mercury trines Saturn and the Sun and Venus trine Neptune in Leo. This describes a nation which is prepared to take risks and is not afraid to speculate. It is a nation which is by its nature confident and optimistic. The Moon in Scorpio and Mars in Capricorn, however, ensure that every risk is a calculated one. An underlying conservatism and thirst for business is

32. Lewis, *Boomerang*, p. 8.
33. Lewis, *Boomerang*, p. 2.
34. Nicholas Campion, *The Book of World Horoscopes*. The chart set for noon – exact time unknown.

reflected here. The ruler of the Sagittarian planets is Jupiter which is conjunct Pluto in Cancer, which denotes not just the industries of generating (Jupiter) power (Pluto) from the land (Cancer) but also the big business (Pluto) of exploring and catching (Jupiter) from their home waters (Cancer). It could also describe the extending (Jupiter) of one nation's (Cancer) banking and financial (Pluto) industry.

On 17 June 1944, when transiting Saturn (at 29° Gemini) and Neptune (at 1° Libra) were square, they picked up the 1918 chart's Mercury (29° Sagittarius)–Pluto (6° Cancer)–Chiron (29° Pisces) T-square. The transiting stellium of Mars, Jupiter and Pluto in Leo triggered the Iceland 1918 position of Neptune in Leo and trined the 1918 Sun and Venus. It was at this time that Iceland's sovereign status was dissolved and it became independent. During this period, Iceland's identity transformed once again: its allegiance with Denmark was completely severed and the country became a republic.

The second chart for Iceland is set for this date at 2pm. This chart has a stellium of Uranus, Mercury, Venus, Sun and Saturn in Gemini in the ninth house showing a growth in education (Iceland has a high number of PhDs per head of population) and where quality education and foreign trade are considered the most highly valued assets of the nation. The Moon in Taurus in the eighth house depicts a nation of people who are 'savings conscious', people of the land and who understand the value of money. The Moon in Taurus is square to Mars in Leo and the Icelandic people have enjoyed a reputation for being aggressive and tough. Michael Lewis, the author of *Boomerang*, describes his experience (quite harshly) with the Icelanders thus: 'We assume they are more or less Scandinavian – a gentle people who just want everyone to have the same amount of everything. They are not. They have a feral streak in them, like a horse that's just pretending to be broken.'[35]

---

35. Lewis, *Boomerang*, p. 23.

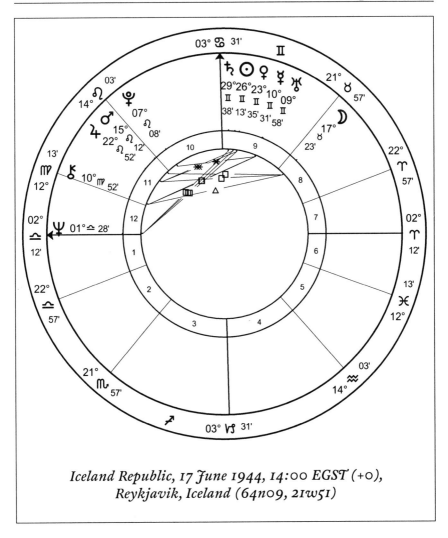

Iceland Republic, 17 June 1944, 14:00 EGST (+0),
Reykjavik, Iceland (64n09, 21w51)

On 6 October 2008, three weeks after the Lehman Brothers bank collapsed, Iceland had an economic meltdown. This was one of the first major banking crises in the world to bring an entire country to its knees. After the Lehman Brothers collapse foreign investors panicked and demanded their capital back from Iceland. When Iceland's Krona devalued, it was unable to pay its creditors. Unlike huge countries and economies such as the US, Iceland did not have a government large or rich enough to bail it out. Over $100 billion was lost in the banking sector, accompanied by an 85 per cent loss in the Icelandic stock market. The losses equated to debts exceeding 850 per cent of GDP (compared to 350 per cent of the US GDP).[36]

The devaluation of assets in Iceland (and its assets abroad) saw the country slide into a dark hole of unprecedented debt. Houses now valued at $500,000 had $1.5 million mortgages on them. Range Rovers worth $35,000 had $100,000 loans against them.[37] The country was officially bankrupt.

On 1 August 2008, the total solar eclipse at 9° Leo triggered Neptune in the 1918 chart and the Moon was only a few hours from completing a conjunction with Pluto in the 1944 chart. In October 2008, Pluto was at its final degree of 29° Sagittarius, and transiting over the 1918 chart's Mercury by conjunction, squaring Chiron (at 29° Pisces) and coming to oppose Pluto (at 6° Libra). Transiting Pluto also opposed the 1944 chart's Sun (26°), Saturn (29°) and Venus (23°) in Gemini, and its MC at 3° Cancer. Pluto on the IC opposing the 1944 Saturn and MC exposes that which has been hidden from everyone, ripping out the foundations on which the new Iceland had built its modern economy, and causing the heads of several banking executives to roll.

From November 2008 until July 2010, Saturn and Uranus were also making a series of oppositions between Virgo/Pisces (18°, 20°, 24° and 28° degrees) and 0° Aries/Libra. This period saw the shocking and totally unpredicted derailing of an entire economy as these planets triggered the mutable stelliums in both Icelandic charts and the angles of the 1944 chart.

Iceland gave us a chilling glimpse into the financial ills of the banking world. It was one of the first examples of how a nation, who had created fake capital by trading assets internally at inflated values,[38] became over-capitalized, played on the flawed international banking system and could

---

36. Lewis, *Boomerang*, p. 3.
37. Lewis, *Boomerang*, p. 8.
38. Lewis, *Boomerang*, p. 17.

be isolated and crippled by a globally accepted system which was ultimately to spin out of control.

Iceland has been used here as an example, as it presents an interesting illustration of how an economy can plunge from golden years to a very dark and impoverished place. Many would argue that the fall of Iceland was due to its own recklessness, but others would say it was merely an unfortunate victim of the wrath of a global tsunami. I tend to think there is an element of truth in both views. Iceland is an example of how economies have been overvalued for the past fifteen years while Pluto has been travelling through Sagittarius and where both national and personal debt has grown exponentially. People and banks have been encouraged to borrow – if not paid to do so – causing the value of assets to deviate from their real value. The sub-prime mortgage crisis highlighted this as Pluto started to make its journey into Capricorn with Jupiter, exposing the consequences of reckless spending and borrowing around the globe, transforming a false golden age to an actual nightmare reality. As Pluto makes its way further into Capricorn to square Uranus, we will undoubtedly see the collapse of many more economies. Of course, Iceland's economic meltdown was not the only unfortunate event that drew global attention to this country. The volcanic ash cloud from the Icelandic volcano Eyjafjallajökull during the week 14–20 April 2010 brought severe disruptions to air travel around the world.

Over the new Moon at 24° Aries as the transiting cardinal T-square of Saturn at 29° Virgo, Uranus at 28° Pisces and Pluto at 5° Capricorn was building, Pluto came to oppose Iceland's 1918 natal Pluto at 6° Cancer. Transiting Uranus and Pluto exactly squared the 1918's Mercury positioned at 29° Sagittarius and picked up Chiron at 29° Pisces.

In the 1944 chart of Iceland, Saturn was travelling over the Ascendant and Neptune was squaring the natal Saturn while Pluto was making a series of conjunctions to the natal IC and Uranus was building towards the country's Descendant.

Besides causing major upheaval in global travel, this particular event also stirred some fear within people. It should also be noted that the new Moon for this chart transposed onto an Astro*Carto*Graphy map ran through Ireland, which was the country most affected by the ash 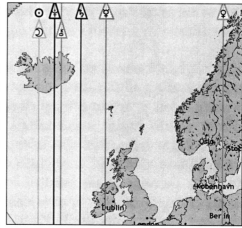 cloud. The event raised questions such as what possible effects could occur if the neighbouring volcano Katla erupted, particularly as the eruption of this volcano historically follows the eruptions of Eyjafjallajökull, as Icelandic President Ólafur Grímsson reminds us.[39] The last time a major eruption occurred was between the years 1821 and 1823. Jupiter was conjunct Pluto at 27° Pisces and square to Uranus–Neptune at 2° Capricorn. Jupiter then conjoined Saturn in June 1821 at 24° Aries. The solar eclipse preceding this was on 14 March 1820, which was conjoined with Pluto, Saturn and Chiron, square to Uranus and Neptune. On the Astro*Carto*Graphy map (above) for this event the eclipse ran directly through the country of Iceland.

Testament to the nature of Uranus–Pluto, natural disasters which humans have no control over become a scary inevitability. Apocalyptic concepts such as severe changes in weather patterns leading to the re-occurrence of ice-age conditions become topical discussions. It is important to note here that these events stir a significant amount of fear within the masses; they are drawn into the experience even though it is occurring halfway around the world. But more importantly, as much as people imagine quite a different world for a short period, these thoughts (and experiences) are fleeting and soon forgotten.

---

39. http://news.bbc.co.uk/1/hi/programmes/newsnight/8631343.stm [accessed 24 March 2012].

Riots Rooted in Inequality

The London Riots
On 6 August 2011, as Uranus and Pluto were square in the sky, Mars in Cancer was making an opposition to Pluto and a square to Uranus in the early degrees of the cardinal signs. At approximately 6:15pm that day, a peaceful protest started in Tottenham Hale. The protest was in support of allegations of injustice in the shooting of Mark Duggan as part of a police operation against gang gun crime within the black community. The peaceful protest had escalated by 8:20pm to a full-scale looting and arson spree throughout London and its suburban areas. This riot lasted four days. Other major towns and cities were also affected. Five people died, sixteen were injured and over £200 million of damage was caused.[40] Over 3,000 people were arrested. There are several debates as to the root cause of the riots and how they escalated, but many agreed that the government had not adequately addressed the consequences of economic crisis and that this helped to fuel them.[41] Mars in T-square with Pluto and Uranus was not only instrumental in sparking a riot in the capital of the UK but also served to stir the anger of the wider population of the UK about the rioters' behaviour.

When Uranus and Pluto make a hard aspect to each other, either by conjunction, square or opposition, the period gives rise to conflict and tension. There will be demands from the people to address social injustice. Uranus will seek to bring about democracy and, when conjunct Pluto, they will jointly strike at the core of the social problem.

Riots of this kind of course are not new. But although strongly linked to global financial crises, they are more

---

40. http://www.bbc.co.uk/news/uk-14532532 [accessed 24 March 2012]; http://www.independent.co.uk/news/uk/crime/the-night-that-rioters-ruled-and-police-lost-control-of-the-streets-of-london-2335067.html [acc. 24 March 2012].
41. http://www.comres.co.uk/polls/Ios_SM_LondonRiots_12thAugust11.pdf [accessed 24 March 2012].

broadly understood in the context of the underpinnings of socio-economic class formation and by addressing the issues of institutionalized inequality. It was reported that over one third of the arrests made from the riots were from youngsters who had been excluded from school.[42] There is something fundamentally wrong about how we look after and accommodate those less fortunate and who are suffering in society. We see links between these riots and the unfolding of events and astrological signatures of previous incidents. To understand how Uranus–Pluto might play out we need to go back and see what happened in previous cycles.

The Civil Rights Movement and Martin Luther King
The Civil Rights Movement campaigned throughout the 1950s and 60s to eradicate racism, to obtain voting rights and economic justice for the black population, and to liberate this section of society from oppression. President Lyndon Johnson (continuing the late President Kennedy's work) signed the Civil Acts Right of 1964 on 2 July.[43] This act introduced the prohibition of racial discrimination in areas such as employment, union membership, accommodation and other publicly funded facilities. It banned discrimination not only on the grounds of race but also on the grounds of sex and religious affiliation. Upon signing the Act, Lyndon shook hands with Martin Luther King. On 6 August 1965, after several further protests for voting rights, Johnson signed the Voting Rights Act of 1965,[44] which provided the opportunity for all black voters to register to vote.

Martin Luther King was the youngest man ever to receive the Nobel Peace Prize on 14 October 1964 for his efforts in the

42. Liz McKeen, *Newsnight*, 16 January 2012
43. http://finduslaw.com/civil_rights_act_of_1964_cra_title_vii_equal_ employment_opportunities_42_us_code_chapter_21 [accessed 24 March 2012].
44. http://searchjustice.usdoj.gov/search?q=crt%20voting%20misc%20 faq&q=site%3Awww.justice.gov%2Fcrt&sort=date%3AD%3AL%3Ad1& output=xml_no_dtd&client=default_frontend&proxystylesheet=default frontend&site=default_collection [accessed 24 March 2012].

Civil Rights Movement, at the time when transiting Uranus was conjunct Pluto and Venus in Virgo and opposing Chiron in Pisces. This was a beautiful point in time, aptly describing the peace (Pisces) and legislation he pushed for so long (Venus) to address social ills (Uranus–Pluto opposing Chiron). This transiting opposition also picked up King's Venus and Moon

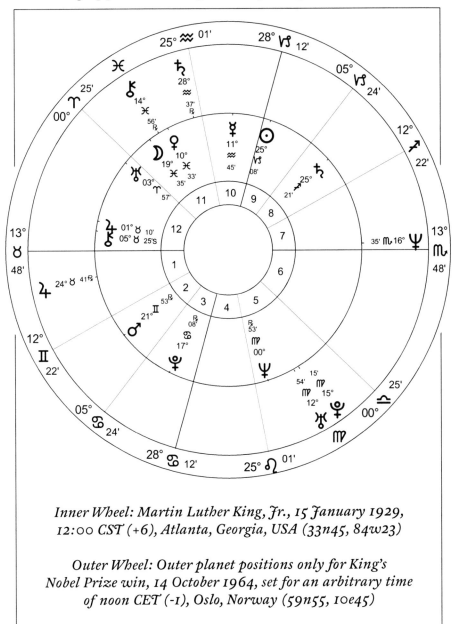

Inner Wheel: Martin Luther King, Jr., 15 January 1929, 12:00 CST (+6), Atlanta, Georgia, USA (33n45, 84w23)

Outer Wheel: Outer planet positions only for King's Nobel Prize win, 14 October 1964, set for an arbitrary time of noon CET (-1), Oslo, Norway (59n55, 10e45)

at 10° and 19° Pisces and squared his Mars at 21° Gemini. For a man who stated he had 'walked to the top of the mountain', this is a wonderful self-description of the Sun in Capricorn on the MC. The man who famously made the 'I have a dream' speech, also had his dream realized by winning the Nobel Prize[45] as Neptune was travelling over his Descendant.

The Watts Riots

The Watts riots began on 11 August 1965. In L.A. a black man was arrested for drunk driving. Within hours, the city area of Watts was filled with protesters and was alight and burning. At the time, some attributed the riots to police brutality, while others blamed soaring hot Californian temperatures, and Cornell Henderson, worker for the Congress of Racial Equality, admitted that 'young hoodlums and agitators... took advantage of the situation for emotional release'.[46] The riots saw the death of 34 people, over 1,000 injuries and $40 million worth of damage. Over 3,000 arrests were made.[47] Reasons for the riots soaring to such an extent were documented by the Governor's Commission of LA who identified their cause to be high unemployment, poor schooling and housing and other inferior living conditions for African Americans.[48] Recommendations and an action plan were formulated to raise the level of employment and living standards, but very few of these recommendations were met.[49]

South Africa and Nelson Mandela

Civil unrest was widespread all over the globe during the mid-1960s. South Africa was experiencing global media

---

45. http://www.nobelprize.org/nobel_prizes/peace/laureates/1964 [accessed 24 March 2012].

46. *Chronicle of the 20th Century*, p. 935.

47. http://mlk-kpp01.stanford.edu/index.php/encyclopedia/encyclopedia/enc_watts_rebellion_los_angeles_1965 [accessed 24 March 2012].

48. http://www.usc.edu/libraries/archives/cityinstress/mccone/contents.html [accessed 24 March 2012].

49. http://articles.latimes.com/1990-07-08/local/me-455_1_watts-riots [accessed 24 March 2012].

coverage highlighting racial segregation by apartheid within the nation. Several political organizations and movements had been formed to address the inequalities experienced by almost 80 per cent of South Africa's population. Since 1948, black South Africans (and Asians) had not been allowed to own land, were stripped of their citizenship, could not vote, had to be segregated from whites on all (poorly serviced) public services and facilities, had to wear cards which identified their racial group, were not permitted to marry or have sex with anyone of a different race, were not permitted into certain white-only public areas, were (poorly) housed in areas of racial groups and were prevented from organising any resistance to the white colonial government.[50] Apartheid was not tolerated by several other countries and, due to their policy of racial exclusion, South Africa was banned from the Olympic Games in Tokyo during the Uranus–Pluto conjunction in 1964. Calls to end apartheid in South Africa were voiced in other countries. An example of this was the protests in New Zealand between 1981 and 1985 which resulted in New Zealand cutting all sporting ties (including rugby) with South Africa until apartheid had been abolished.[51]

Nelson Mandela was an anti-apartheid activist and leader of the ANC's (African National Congress's) armed wing. He was sentenced to life in prison on 12 June 1964 for sabotaging and plotting to overthrow the South African government by revolution. He served 27 years until he was released from prison on 11 February 1990 and his release was broadcast all over the globe.[52] His efforts in reform and creating equality in this nation led to him being elected its President, an election in which all citizens of South Africa, almost 20,000,000 people,

---

50. http://www.sahistory.org.za/pages/chronology/thisday/representation-of-natives-act.htm [accessed 24 March 2012]; http://africanhistory.about.com/library/bl/blsalaws.htm [accessed 24 March 2012].
51. http://www.nzhistory.net.nz/culture/1981-springbok-tour [accessed 24 March 2012].
52. http://century.guardian.co.uk/1990-1999/Story/0,,112389,00.html [accessed 24 March 2012].

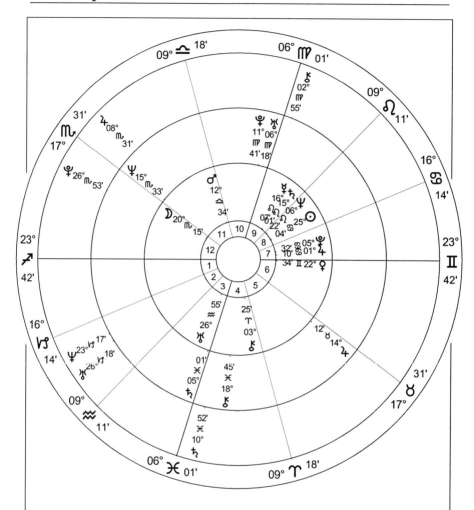

*Inner Wheel: Nelson Mandela, 18 July 1918, 'afternoon',
rectified by Noel Tyl to 14:54 EET (-2),
Umtata, South Africa (31s35, 28e47)*

*Middle Wheel: Outer planet positions only for Mandela's
imprisonment, 12 June 1964, set for an arbitrary time of
noon EET (-2), Pretoria, South Africa (25s45, 28e10)*

*Outer Wheel: Outer planet positions only for Mandela's
Presidential inauguration, 10 May 1994, set for an arbitrary
time of noon EET (-2), Pretoria, South Africa (25s45, 28e10)*

were permitted to cast their vote for the very first time.[53] He was the first black President and his inauguration occurred on 10 May 1994. This event was monumental for South Africa and the rest of the world as it brought to global attention the emancipation of millions of people who had suffered great oppression for almost half a century. The 1993 Nobel Peace Prize was awarded jointly to Nelson Mandela and Frederik Willem de Klerk (the previous President) 'for their work for the peaceful termination of the apartheid regime, and for laying the foundations for a new democratic South Africa'.[54]

As we can see from the tri-wheel (inner wheel, Mandela's chart; middle wheel, his imprisonment; and the outer wheel, his inauguration as President), on the day of Mandela's imprisonment transiting Uranus and Pluto were conjunct the MC of Mandela's natal chart (opposing Saturn and the IC), illustrating the public exposure of his underground involvement and forced enclosure in prison. These outer planets on his angles also reflect the international acknowledgement and respect he gained, as well as indicate that he was made the scapegoat for his people. Transiting Mars is square his natal Uranus in Aquarius, highlighting the crime, violence and struggle for emancipation of the masses. Additionally, transiting Jupiter (in the sixth house) is opposite Neptune (eleventh house) and picking up Mandela's Moon in Scorpio in the twelfth house, perhaps indicative of his sacrifice, heroism and tireless work towards highlighting the dark sickness that had permeated the country and oppressed several millions of people for almost five decades.

It is important to note that this is a rectified chart[55] and should be considered speculative. However, it does appear to be an excellent rectification. From the transits of Mandela's inauguration as President we can see that Saturn in Pisces

53. http://electionresources.org/za/provinces.php?election=1994 [accessed 24 March 2012].
54. http://www.nobelprize.org/nobel_prizes/peace/laureates/1993 [accessed 24 March 2012].
55. Rectified by Noel Tyl from a statement of 'afternoon'. See 'Birth Data'.

arrives back to make a series of conjunctions to the position of Saturn at the time he was imprisoned (his term in prison being a full Saturn cycle), and again opposes the 1964 Uranus–Pluto conjunction. Thus, the 1994 chart is a Saturn return (in Pisces) for the 1964 chart and, again, Saturn is travelling opposite Mandela's natal MC – a time for rebuilding and acknowledging sacrifices and the past and reminding us of the darkness and suffering that had been experienced before this event. Saturn returns are about 'moving on', learning from what has gone before and making the necessary steps to press forward. We also see transiting Pluto opposing Mars on the date of his imprisonment, as well as squaring Mandela's natal Uranus, creating a T-square, here representing the overturning of violence and highlighting the victory of the people and the promise of a new dawn for a nation as it strives to re-invent itself as a collective community. Transiting Uranus and Neptune in Capricorn are in opposition to Mandela's natal Sun in Cancer, possibly reflective of the past and the potential internal conflict he will continue to carry as President. The nation labelled Mandela 'father' and this is aptly described by these natal and transit points too.

The LA Riots and Rodney King
On 3 March 1991, Rodney Glenn King was beaten by four police officers after a high-speed motor pursuit. This incident was caught on video tape by a neighbour. The officers in question were put on trial for police brutality but were acquitted by a jury. As a result of the acquittal, a mass riot, known as the 1992 Los Angeles Riots, broke out at 5pm on 29 April 1992 amongst the black community and lasted for six days. Assault, arson and looting were rampant during this period, which saw the death of 53 people. Thousands more were injured and over $1 billion worth of damage was done.

Rodney King was born on 2 April 1965 and has Uranus conjunct Pluto in his natal chart. King was also born with Mars conjunct these planets and Mars also the dispositor of his Aries stellium of Venus, Sun, Moon and Mercury. Mars,

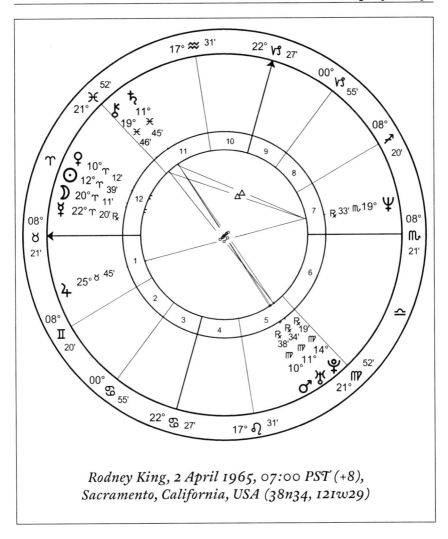

Rodney King, 2 April 1965, 07:00 PST (+8),
Sacramento, California, USA (38n34, 121w29)

Uranus and Pluto in Virgo are in opposition to Saturn and
Chiron in Pisces and his Neptune is placed in Scorpio in the
seventh house opposing Jupiter rising in Taurus in the first
house.

King was not a stranger to violent crime in his life and at the
time of his beating was on parole for a robbery in which he had
used an iron bar to threaten the store owner. *The Independent's*
headlines on 21 February 1993 read, 'As he awaits a new trial
of the police who beat him, Rodney King has become a hero,
a demon, and a gold mine'.

King's chart is interesting as he was a central figure in the Los Angeles riots. He was certainly not the cause of them but his stellium of Mars, Uranus and Pluto opposing Saturn and Chiron in Pisces definitely describes a victim (Pisces) of brutality (Mars, Uranus and Pluto).

If we look at the tri-wheel (opposite page) of King's natal chart (inner wheel) along with the time of the beating (middle wheel) and then the time when the LA riots broke out (outer wheel) we can view the transits that were taking place at each of these events. At the time of the beating there was a transiting Jupiter–Saturn opposition in the sky which will always bring rise to social change and cause social institutions (such as the police) to come under scrutiny in some way. There was also a Uranus–Neptune conjunction in Capricorn, perhaps bringing some unpredictable disillusionment with authority. This conjunction was trine King's stellium in Virgo. Transiting Mars, the planet of war, becomes the apex of a T-square as it is squaring King's natal stellium in Virgo and his Saturn and Chiron in Pisces, describing the act of violence and victimization.

Transiting Pluto was travelling through King's natal seventh house, about to conjoin his Neptune in Scorpio and was approaching an opposition to his Jupiter in Taurus in the first house, Jupiter being King's eighth-house ruler. The Jupiter–Pluto opposition between the first and seventh houses illustrates the bullying and violation, and with Pluto on King's Neptune in Scorpio in the seventh house, along with transiting Neptune about to conjoin King's MC, perhaps denotes the recording of the video tape by a hidden witness. It is important to note here that Neptune has not yet reached the MC (the public arena) and the tape was not fully shown until Neptune had actually passed this point.

The outer wheel is set for the time of when the LA riots broke out – the same day as the acquittal of the four policemen, thirteen months after the beating occurred. One of the most prominent points to note in this chart is that Jupiter has now

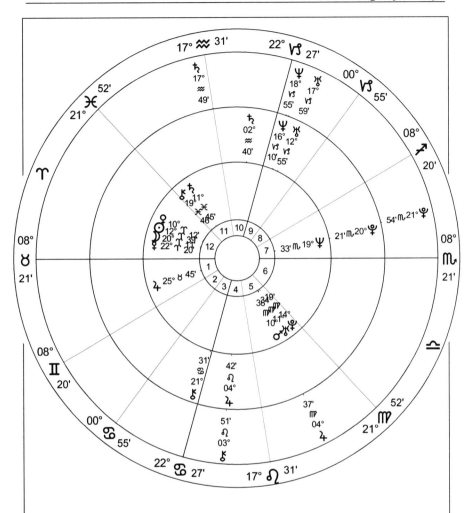

Inner Wheel: Rodney King, 2 April 1965, 07:00 PST (+8), Sacramento, California, USA (38n34, 121w29)

Middle Wheel: Outer planet positions only for King's police beating, 3 March 1991, 00:53 PST (+8), Los Angeles, California, USA (34n03, 118w14)

Outer Wheel: Outer planet positions only for the LA Riots, 29 April 1992, 17:00 PDT (+7), Los Angeles, California, USA (34n03, 118w14)

come to conjoin King's stellium of Mars, Uranus and Pluto. Although on this date it sits at 4° Virgo, Jupiter had started its transit over the stellium in November 1991 when it became exact with King's Mars; it had travelled over the stellium, gone retrograde and went direct after four months on 30 April – within 24 hours of the riots starting.

Transiting Chiron was within a degree of the position (3° Leo) of Jupiter at the time of the beating (4° Leo and opposing the Saturn from that same date at 2° Aquarius).

What is so interesting about these charts is that Rodney King was born with the Uranus–Pluto conjunction also conjunct Mars. Mars is about anger, conflict and fighting – but also about initiation and courage. His beating depicts a time when he was victimized by a physically violent act (transiting Mars creating a T-square with his natal planets) and at the time of the riots, an event where his own personal experience became *the* reason for firing up the masses in their quest for social justice and equality. He was the epicentre of this event. The naive and warriorlike Mars does not think about the consequences or the collateral damage of its actions: the high-speed motor pursuit of King, the police brutality, the jury's quick decision, and then the violent damage of the riots, were all examples of this.

This is a sequence of events where there has been an angry and irrational acting out, with those involved not thinking or preparing for the consequences. At the time of the riots, Uranus in Capricorn is sextile to Pluto in Scorpio and the sextile is also picking up transiting Neptune and King's MC by conjunction. This is an example of how the 1960s' civil rights protests and calls for equality were brought under the spotlight again, by a man born under the Uranus–Pluto conjunction, at the time of the first major aspect Uranus and Pluto made following their conjunction – the sextile. However, instead of Virgo, these planets resided in Capricorn and Scorpio and this situation was about abuse of power and authority, exposed to the public only because somebody had filmed it (Neptune). In a civil case in LA on 19 April 1994, King won and was awarded $3.8 million in damages as Neptune (at 23°) had just passed his MC, bringing the truth of the matter and the full exposure of the video tape to the public. He was having his Saturn return in Pisces, acknowledging and correcting the victimization he had suffered. Transiting Saturn (at 9° Pisces) trined Jupiter in the sky (at 11° Scorpio), reflecting social justice being somewhat restored, and transiting Jupiter in Scorpio conjoined King's descendant, representing 'the payout' and also perhaps the (future) romantic entanglement and then engagement to one of the jurors serving on this case.[56]

These examples bring our attention to the inequalities of race and culture that, until the Uranus–Pluto conjunction in Virgo in the 1960s, were tolerated by many. What these events did was to challenge and then ultimately transform the perception of the masses, purging a sick ideology that permeated society.

This event is a prime example of the nature of the Uranus–Pluto conjunction, what it stands for and how it is acted out. It also represents the events happening on the first major aspect these planets make – the sextile – after the initial conjunction. As Uranus makes its squares to Pluto over the next few years we can expect such concerns to be stirred up and escalated again with further riots and protests regarding inequality - building with the squares.

In May 2011, as the Uranus and Pluto square approached, there were news reports in the UK about the trial for the murder of Stephen Lawrence, a 19-year old black teenager who was stabbed to death in 1993, in what was understood to be a racially-motivated murder. Due to a new law being introduced, two suspects who had previously been acquitted were allowed to stand trial again; this time they were convicted

---

56. Second Printing Addition: Sadly, King was found dead on 17 June 2012, just seven days before the first of the current set of Uranus–Pluto squares.

of his murder.[57] This new law could help to prosecute criminals who were previously protected by double-jeopardy legislation, and other previously acquitted suspects may be forced to stand trial again if enough evidence is brought to light against them.

The 1960s era saw capitalism, anti-democratic issues and inequality being addressed and, as the Uranus–Pluto conjunction occurred, redress to these issues was sought through revolutionary action and protests. Many changes were executed within social structures, such as legislation, education and employment, to address and avoid further inequalities and to change people's world view. Positive changes are marked by the increase of mixed marriages; multiculturalism has increased throughout the western world and many more children throughout the world are being born into a rich variety of mixed cultural backgrounds. Some positive steps were taken during the Uranus–Pluto sextile in the mid-1990s but the further, more problematic issues are of the same nature as those of the 60s: institutionalized racism. However, as much as these issues have been addressed, we are still faced with the evident and ensuing problems that will continue to surface. Issues of racial prejudice and identity and conflicting ideas and feelings regarding cultural assimilation (as opposed to integration) will undoubtedly be raised as the upcoming Uranus–Pluto squares form.

57. http://www.dailymail.co.uk/news/article-2079782/Stephen-Lawrence-trial-Gary-Dobson-David-Norris-guilty-murder.html [accessed 1 February 2012].

A Vision of the Near Future

Economic Failings, Aftershocks and Changes
When people ask me what I think will happen with the Uranus–Pluto squares, my answer is always the same: we have yet to see the full impact of what happened from the cardinal crisis in 2010. Although Uranus and Pluto were not yet exactly square at that point, they were within a small orb and, along with Mars, Jupiter and Saturn, started the wide-sweeping changes – both natural and man-made – that followed. The damage has now already been done, we just haven't seen the consequences of it all yet, and the Uranus–Pluto squares will be felt like aftershocks of a situation that has already crumbled.

Whether it is a financial catastrophe, conflict over inequalities or an event of an environmental nature, the first punch has already been thrown; but the fight is far from over. As Uranus and Pluto start to make their squares we will begin to see the unfolding of what first occurred in 2010, and the future outcomes that it will bring.

Like a house that has had a demolition ball run through it – smack! right through the centre – the foundations are now completely weak but the house still remains standing. While we all try to patch up the interior and exterior of the house, sealing the cracks, mending the broken glass and replacing the bent doors, as time goes by, and with every passing square between Uranus and Pluto, the house will experience further tremors. Gradually, there will be more closed doors and uninhabitable rooms – it is only a matter of time before it completely crumbles. Exactly when this will happen, nobody is sure. There are many who do not want to look at the foundations, nor want to understand the engineering structure of the property, or just don't believe the inevitable will happen. There is only one certainty and that is that the house will fall – it will crumble to the ground. When it does, nobody will be surprised. What is yet to be debated and discussed is why and how this happened in the first place – conflict will arise over who actually owns the crane, hitched up the demolition ball and who drove it through the house, but the arguments may never be fully resolved.

What we do know is that, as people lose faith in existing methods of capitalism and are unable to trust the financial institutions and governments that have provided a security blanket for so many decades (even centuries), new systems of economics across the board will be required. It would be sensible for debt to be restructured as populations and nations will be less able to pay back debt. Debt is a claim on future money and future employment, and given the rising rates of unemployment there is a need to become very aware of the fact that the future can no longer be expected to be more prosperous than the present and that a lot of debt will actually never be able to be repaid. Much talk has already been had on the debt the next generation will inherit and this becomes more likely with debts escalating around the globe.

How this debt can be restructured is too large a subject to go into in this section, and best left to those qualified to do so, but there will undoubtedly be speculation in the next few years, during the Uranus–Pluto square, on how this can be done. The likelihood of restructuring debt by downsizing it proportionately would ease up the challenges for individuals and for countries. But the likelihood is that the end-user will pay for the debt by increases in taxes and negative incentives like 50-year mortgages,[58] which have previously been implemented in Japan, where people will be locked into debt repayment for several decades, bequeathing their mortgages rather than their assets to their children. This kind of economic reshuffle could add further difficulty if innovations such as disposable housing become a feature in the near future. Properties which are increasingly being built from renewable sources (such as hemp) could transfer

---

58. Wendy Stacey, 'The Property Market Lecture', London School of Astrology, 19 October 2008.

housing from the previous bricks and mortar fixed asset to a disposable and more environmentally friendly one. This is only a small example but one that exemplifies the struggle and crossroads we are faced with.

Pluto in Capricorn brings some advancement to architecture and Uranus in Aries wants things to change and move toward greater simplicity. Kevin McCloud, television presenter of *Grand Designs* in the UK, built a house made from renewable resources on a shoestring in just seven days.[59] Something like disposable housing could have a huge impact on land prices around the globe (coupled with travel time shortening and people being able to work remotely). Pluto in Capricorn is also concerned with land; Uranus in Aries is about changing the goalposts.

New forms of investing will ensue and we can see the start of this happening. Uranus–Pluto is about equality and innovation and we can see a new type of *Dragons' Den* being organized online, where people with money can back other people's innovations, inventions and start-up business enterprises. These are early days and while the concept remains honest and legitimate, sites such as Indigo, Crowd Surfing and Crowdcube are examples of how people can invest and interact with each other without intermediaries taking any cut and where the process is self-regulating.

There will be a change in the way we make financial transactions. With the introduction of the ATM in 1967,[60] cash and plastic cards changed the way people made monetary transactions. Now, phones and cards have almost replaced cash, and with the implementation of Pluto in Capricorn's 'big brother' foothold, we will see the growth of fingerprinting and electronic chipping as methods of payment.

---

59. *The Radio Times*, 3 May 2008.
60. The first ATM machine in the world opened on 27 June 1967 at the Enfield branch of Barclays Bank, see http://news. bbc. co. uk/1/hi/6230194. stm [accessed 25 January 2012].

The 2011 film, *In Time*, is an interesting representation of not just how time has become the new currency (Pluto in Capricorn) but also gives us some insight into how the future may look, with humans being chipped with devices that can credit and debit our 'accounts'. There is a move away from traditional investments such as banking and savings, pension schemes and the stock market; the investment in gold is already changing rapidly and has been since the 2010 cardinal climax, as the faith in the old capitalistic systems started to crumble. People are now investing in new ways, such as Bitcoin (an electronic cash system using social networking), and starting to lend to each other through online sites rather than going through intermediaries such as banks. Such radical shifts in the way people make, use and measure their money or wealth will also affect social mobility and, with new opportunities, will bring new ways to climb the economic ladder.

Threat of Pandemics
One reason why cash will cease to be used may possibly be attributed to some infectious disease (real or not), when the 20°–25° areas of Taurus and Aquarius are hit again, as they were during the outbreak of 'mad-cow' disease, bird flu, SARS, foot and mouth disease and then swine flu in 2007. Taurus rules our four-legged creatures and Aquarius those that fly. The next period which could trigger this is from March 2023 to April 2025, as Uranus makes the journey through the later degrees of Taurus, Pluto enters Aquarius and Neptune moves out of Pisces and into Aries.

Outer planets moving through the final degrees of a sign and the first degrees of the next sign are quite often at their most potent. When a planet is on its way out of the sign it has occupied for a long period, there is often an event that marks the symbolism of that planet in the final degrees of that sign. Similarly, when an outer planet ingresses into the next sign, it is raw, fresh and bursting with possibilities, and this is also often marked by an event that has the signature of that particular planet in that specific sign.

Another interesting date will be when Saturn ingresses into Scorpio on 5 October 2012. This particular ingress has Saturn exactly conjunct Mercury. The ruler, Mars, is at the final degree of Scorpio and is the apex of a T-square with Neptune at 0° and Chiron at 5° (both retrograde) in Pisces and with Venus at 3° Virgo. The Moon during the ingress is exactly conjunct Jupiter at 16° Gemini. The health of individuals and nations (again, real or not) will become a focus, and this picks up the UK's 1801 chart, with Pluto at 7° Capricorn exactly squaring the UK's Ascendant–Descendant axis at 7° Libra–Aries. Neptune and Chiron also pick up the 1801 Pluto at 2° Pisces.

The last ingress of Saturn into Scorpio was conjunct Pluto (in Libra) in 1983, when the newly discovered AIDS and HIV virus shocked the globe. We also saw the exposure of sexual abuse stories on an international scale. Both Pluto and Scorpio symbolize sex, death and trust issues, and these areas were brought to people's attention. The 2012 ingress of Saturn into Scorpio is conjunct Mercury and will also bring matters of sexuality to the foreground, and Mercury will bring to the conjunction a new message for the people. Mercury is about how we interact, how things are transferred; it is not a planet that is related to intimacy – it is concerned with more mental stimulus and points of enquiry. Without wishing to sound too far-fetched, the film *The Demolition Man* comes to mind. It shows a vision of the future in which people have sex 'virtually' rather than physically, in order to eradicate the spread of disease. With this future line-up, Neptune in Pisces, and technological innovations coupled with paranoia about epidemics and pandemics, this concept does not seem so implausible. The Saturn ingress will also be followed by a solar eclipse on 13 November 2012, with the Sun and Moon conjunct at 21° Scorpio, echoing the economic and sexual themes here.

With people now largely meeting potential partners through online services and speed-dating, we have easy and fast access to new friends and lovers. However, in the technological revolution that we are living in, physical and verbal interaction is decreasing. Children in school playgrounds at lunchtimes are participating less in exercise and personal interaction, while spending more time texting or playing with their electronic games. This comes at a large cost to human interaction and subsequently to real intimacy. Following from this we can expect an increase in loneliness and depression. With Neptune entering Pisces we will see more and more of this in our younger generations. The ability to 'connect' to each other will transform from a real one to a virtual one. Each day, virtual worlds are becoming more and more popular. There are already millions of people around the world who interact through Internet games and virtual recreation by creating a virtual self. These virtual selves are normally more attractive, more talented and wealthier than our real selves – they are what we aspire to be, and may soon become who we think we are. Virtual selves will be role models for the next generation, and along with other technological devices will be a contributing source of addiction and depression.

Interesting Dates
Below are some interesting dates that will possibly catch our attention over the coming years. They do not of course take all outer planetary configurations into account (that would require another book!). There are several other periods over the next few years, besides the seven Uranus–Pluto squares, that will show both positive and challenging times ahead, as well as other aspects that will occur, and other techniques we can use, such as eclipses and stationary points that can be explored. It is also too lengthy to look at all the countries and how they can be affected by the Uranus–Pluto squares and other configurations that will occur in the near future.

Another interesting time will be January to May 2014, when Jupiter (at 11°–15° Cancer) will link to the Uranus–Pluto square. It is important to note that Jupiter's position will pick up the UK's Sun in the 1801 chart at 10° Capricorn and the US Sibly chart Sun at 13° Cancer. When the Sun in a nation's chart is triggered, it so often represents the leader of that country. The Sun also represents the nation's confidence and Uranus–Pluto will see a squeeze put on these nations, possibly with lending, quantitative easing (printing money) and debt management in general. Pluto in Capricorn opposing Jupiter in Cancer will bring an end to extended overdrafts, but the square to Uranus in Aries will hopefully bring a new way of managing this. Jupiter in Cancer is also about protecting the home and therefore homeland security will be spotlighted in some way during this period. Jupiter often brings legal issues to the fore and, opposing Pluto and squaring Uranus, there may be some accountability and transparency issues raised. Jupiter likes scandals as well, and Pluto is conjoined with Venus during this time, which could also bring up issues with women in some way. Mercury is conjunct Neptune in the sign of Pisces for the first time in over one hundred and fifty years, so this period is certainly indicative of a scandal on a large scale.

As mentioned previously in this book, when outer planets transit the degrees of the Uranus–Pluto conjunction in the 1960s, which are 16° and 17° Virgo, some areas that relate to that 60s period will be triggered in some way. In February and March 2015, Chiron arrives at 16° Pisces – the degree opposing the Uranus–Pluto conjunction of the 1960s. It should also be emphasized that not only is Chiron triggering that degree but also it will happen during the time of the last of the seven exact Uranus–Pluto squares. In addition, fifty years previously, Chiron was also opposing the Uranus–Pluto conjunction, and now it returns to the same degree while Uranus and Pluto make their last square. This will be an interesting period with issues from the 1960s arising again, with Chiron spotlighting the underdog and civil unrest again as a focus. Neptune also squares Saturn, and with Chiron in Pisces we might start to see panic about water shortages and long hidden (or forgotten) inequalities that begin permeate the consciousness of society. This period also speaks of 'spreads' or some form of 'contamination' and will be a reminder of the natural resources of the planet we need to look after.

Between May 2018 and February 2020, Neptune will travel several times over 16° and 17° Pisces – exactly opposite the degree of the Uranus–Pluto conjunction. Again, this will bring attention to certain ills in society and highlight health on micro and macro levels. Water will be a focus and revolutionary solutions will hopefully come forward to global problems. This period may also correlate with the meltdown of initiatives that were put into place under the Uranus–Pluto conjunction of the 1960s. There may be a redressing of those ideas that never worked before, and a revisiting of these areas by looking at them from different and new perspectives.

There is an interesting solar eclipse that occurs on 9 March 2016. The New Moon chart that follows (set for London) has the Sun and Moon at 18° Pisces, conjoined with Chiron, opposing Jupiter and square to Saturn in Sagittarius on the Ascendant. Although the Uranus–Pluto square will be 'officially' over by then, these planets are still less than two degrees from squaring each other. This chart has five planets in Pisces and with an apex of Saturn in Sagittarius there is an 'underground' feel to this period. Something buried or otherwise unseen could gain some attention. Jupiter is prominent in this chart as it is the most elevated planet and ruler of the apex, stellium and the chart (set for London). Here, travel links from the Underground, National Rail, to the Thames or even the M25 (the great orbital motorway surrounding London), or the South and North Circular (the smaller orbital roads surrounding London) will come under the radar. If we compare this with the UK 1801 chart, Mercury at 18° Sagittarius is picked up here in hard aspect. Mercury in the 1801 chart resides in Sagittarius in the third house, so travel within the UK is emphasized. Postal systems and road and train links will become a focus. The media, education systems and security from new viruses over the Internet could all play a part in this. It does not of course have to be a negative manifestation, as with much Jupiter and Pisces and an optimistically-placed Mercury in the 1801 chart, there is opportunity for creative innovations.

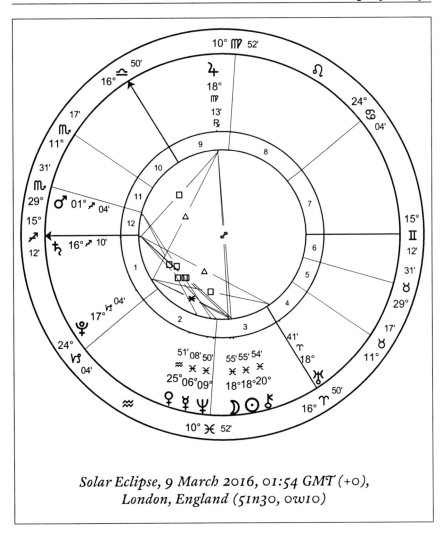

Solar Eclipse, 9 March 2016, 01:54 GMT (+0),
London, England (51n30, 0w10)

Beyond 2020

Another fascinating time to live through will be when Pluto makes its journey into Aquarius in 2024 and, only a few years earlier, Jupiter and Saturn will have made a conjunction in this sign (this is the first conjunction of Jupiter and Saturn in Aquarius in an unbroken sequence in 960 years). The conjunction cycle of these planets moves from the Earth element into the Air element, which may create the platform which will lead us out of a materialistic culture into a mental one and lead to a period when we will embark on a more technologically advanced society which parallels something along the lines of *Star Trek*.

On 26 January 1842, Jupiter and Saturn made a conjunction at 8°54′ Capricorn and since this date (except 1980) all conjunctions have been in the Earth element. This period saw the introduction of new markets and the escalation of capitalism. Congruent with the element of Earth, this period has seen materialism soar, the planet stripped of its natural resources and consumption (and subsequently waste) has grown to unprecedented levels.

As these social planets continue to travel through the Earth element, people tend to be more anchored, heavier, and more concerned with the present. Earth is a very dense but realistic element and is concerned with boundaries and regulation. While Jupiter and Saturn travel through the Earth triplicity, society has become interested in hard work, in what can be owned, measured and exploited; it has focused on the resources that are available. It has encouraged an ideology that is interested in growth, particularly economic and, through the desire for a 'better standard of life', wants to have more – which can often be at the expense of others (society). This is about to radically change in 2024, when Jupiter and Saturn enter a new era and spearhead us (along with Pluto) into an exciting but scary cyber world.

Further commentary on Uranus square Pluto forecasts can be found on Wendy Stacey's website www.wendystacey.com/ UranusSquarePluto

Back To the Future – Towards a Virgo Society

To understand the up and coming Uranus–Pluto squares we need to go back to the beginning of the cycle and think not only about what occurred at its seed but also how the first part of the cycle has unfolded. This can give us some idea of the evolution of society and how we build and live our lives today.

As astrologers we understand that cycles do not operate in isolation. However, in this chapter, I would like to narrow the context of the subject under consideration. Uranus and Pluto travelled through Virgo for most of the 60s. Often when we think about these planets, particularly their conjunction, we look mainly at the planets themselves, studying the cycle and their characteristics. We rarely consider the sign of Virgo, the sign they tenanted during this period. This chapter aims to take a glimpse at what has happened since the 1960s, what this period and the generation born of the 60s has brought forth and the changes it has made within our society.[61]

Keywords for Virgo:

> Helpful, Unassuming, Dependable, Analytical, Service-orientated, Soft, Malleable, Adaptable, Self-reliant, Fussy, Shy, Modest, Humble, Critical, Perfectionist, Conservative, Practical, Diligent, Meticulous, Intelligent, Discreet, Reserved, Exacting, Feminine, Physical, Persistent.

---

61. It is also important to note that, due to short and long ascension, the northern hemisphere will have a significantly higher proportion of people born with Virgo rising than the southern hemisphere.

Those born in this era are a generation in pursuit of perfection where every social institution has either undergone a radical change to incorporate Virgo qualities or has been formed with the sign's traits. This extends to how we work, our concept of our bodies, the way in which we conduct our daily lives, organize our homes and families, our interests and leisure and the way we perceive the world. If we explore how these characteristics have been incorporated since the last conjunction, we can see that they also have an impact and may offer the opportunity for change or crises as the current cardinal Uranus–Pluto squares unfold.

Virgo Characteristics and the Maiden

Virgo is a mutable Earth sign, ruled by the planet Mercury, and has the virgin maiden as its symbol – it is the only sign in the zodiac to be represented by a female image.

Virgo is a practical sign, and one of Virgo's main characteristics is the desire to master everything it does. Virgos have an eye for detail and a critical and analytical perspective. They seek to understand the mechanics of what makes things work by dissecting them into their separate components, both physically and mentally. Virgos have both a practical know-how and a down-to-earth approach, and are happy to put in the physical effort needed to get matters completed. But natives of the sign also require intellectual stimulation and intelligent dialogue. Typical Virgos are known for being complex characters with a witty, wry and slightly cynical take on life. Virgos like to engineer their physical environment as well as situations, and work to ensure that everything operates properly, efficiently and in a functional way. They use their talents to improve situations and are happiest when serving the needs of others.

Easily irritated by imperfection, Virgos seek to improve everything they touch, to make it as faultless and flawless as possible — a never-ending and often stressful task. Virgos continually work to fix everything around them. Virgos are also known for wanting to help and be of service. They take a great deal of pleasure and satisfaction from being needed, and for this reason they like to make themselves useful to others. Unafraid of hard work and possessed with a strong sense of responsibility, Virgos can often find themselves in the position of martyrs, taking on too many tasks and often believing they can do a better job than anyone else. This is often true, but quite obsessive when you have many people with Virgo planets in one place, or a whole generation with Uranus and Pluto conjunct in Virgo. One of the sign's main motivations is the need to achieve, and Virgos can be fuelled by a fear of under-achievement or failure to do a less than perfect job. So, working hard, having something to do and performing well are major drives for natives of this sign.

As an Earth sign, Virgo is concerned with the natural, tangible, physical and material realm. Thus the body, health and nutritional matters are principal concerns for the sign. Virgos are often preoccupied with their own health as well as that of others, which can often turn into a tendency to hypochondria, superstition and anxiety. This obsessive thinking can often lead to natives of the sign becoming prone to despair and despondency, and the idealistic Virgo maiden can frequently retreat into herself, closing herself off from others when worried, disappointed or hurt.

The symbol of the Virgin stands with a sheaf of wheat in her hand. The sheaf represents the harvest of wheat and agriculture, as well as wisdom. Virgo is associated with wisdom and experience, but it can also have a naïve quality. Virgos are often more concerned with the present than the future, and although they are able to weigh up any risks involved in the projects they undertake, they do not always anticipate the end result. The sign is attributed with the quality of insight based on what has been learned through experience, but it does not always possess sufficient foresight or see the larger scheme of things.

In Greek mythology Virgo is often associated with Demeter, the Earth Mother and mother of Persephone. Demeter was responsible for regulating the seasons and ruled over nature and its cycles, as well as domestic duties. Virgo holds a matriarchal position as the most feminine of all the signs and represents the quintessential goddess, encapsulating all that is female.

Virgo is a mutable and therefore adaptable sign. Virgos can be happy to work for and around others and are sensitive to their environment and concerned with environmental issues. Lovers of nature, and all that is pure and natural, they tend to be concerned with the cycles of nature over which the sign presides. They are typically caring and demure individuals, shy and easily embarrassed.

In Christian symbolism we find the Virgin Mary. The ultimate matriarch of Christianity is an icon of all that is pure and moral. The young maiden who gave birth to God's son is believed to have conceived him through a miracle while still a virgin. A servant and saint, revered for her purity and innocence and unstained by sin, has been regarded as the ultimate image of the feminine for much of western society during the last two thousand years. Her perfect being, chaste and subservient to the Divine, became an integral part of society's expectations of women, and particularly unmarried girls.

When the Uranus–Pluto conjunction occurred in Virgo in 1965 and 1966, there was an unprecedented sexual revolution which challenged the myth of the Blessed Virgin and the values of virginity and sexual abstinence that she stood for. Pluto is associated with sexuality and Uranus with freedom. Sexual freedom, experimentation and expression become synonymous with the 1960s, as represented by the Summer of Love in San Francisco in 1967. This period brought a new wave of feminism, and a new representation of the maiden unfolded as women regained control over their bodies and their sexuality. The Blessed Virgin was replaced with a new maiden ideology, a new set of attitudes and feminist theories. She became associated with equality and independence. She declared control over her own body and sexual behaviour as well as her own child-bearing propensities, aided by the invention of the contraceptive pill, which liberated women from this point onwards. Women could now decide when they wanted to have sex and with whom, and could delay (or permanently avoid) pregnancy and family life if they chose to do so. For the first time the maiden could choose between work, health and motherhood as she so desired.

Virgo is probably one of the most unappreciated and undervalued signs of the zodiac. The generation who was born and lived through the 1960s era carries with it the forgotten treasures of the maiden. The qualities of Virgo are acted out but not always consciously, and they are rarely embraced or revered. The explosive Uranus–Pluto conjunction which occupied the sign and led to the sexual revolution in the 1960s has also paved the way for the characteristics of Virgo to subtly become dominant and permeate the very fabric of our society, without us realizing it.

Work

Virgo is the zodiac sign that rules work. Work describes what we have to do, the means and sacrifices we make in order to sustain ourselves. What we do in our work defines us in many ways, and how we do it tells us about our attitudes and approaches to work. Virgo, on a mundane level, represents the masses and the working class. It describes issues of the workplace, employment or unemployment. When Uranus and Pluto were conjunct in Virgo, they brought major shifts to the meaning of work, how people conducted themselves in the workplace and the requirements of their jobs.

Since the 1960s much of the developed world has experienced a rapid and huge transformation of work and employment in a way that has never been seen before in human history. Virgo is about service, and since the Uranus–Pluto conjunction work in the western world has transformed from a predominantly product-based to a service-based environment. The service industry is now the largest and fastest growing sector of our economy. Areas of public health and hospitals, government, transportation, education, waste disposal, financial and legal services, consulting, media and news, hospitality in all forms, tourism, real estate, retail and wholesale are industries which have grown exponentially in the past few decades (of course other cycles would have also contributed to this).

Product-based environments have now been transferred abroad where there are cheaper labour costs, and the service industries in the developed countries are no longer able to compete with the labour markets of the developing world.

Researchers Abrams and Astill (2001) traced an ordinary pair of Lee Cooper jeans from the denim washing process in Tunisia all the way to Milan where the material is spun and dyed using German dyes made in Frankfurt. The cotton itself comes mainly from Benin where, typically, day labourers earn the equivalent of 60p and peasant farmers can earn £15 profit from 1.5 tonnes of cotton. The cotton for the pockets of the jeans is grown in Pakistan, and while the zip tape comes from France, the zip teeth are from Japan. The brass poppers are made in Germany from Namibian and Australian copper.[62]

Thus, a pair of Lee Cooper jeans is an example of global markets, and the success of this particular product can be attributed to access to foreign raw materials, dependency on fixed currency markets and arguably the exploitation of skilled and cheap labour in other countries.

This type of manufacturing has developed since the 1960's Uranus–Pluto conjunction in Virgo, and with the current square in the cycle between these two planets, this labour process and work in general will come under the radar again. Work that is outsourced abroad, be it manufacturing or new increased services such as call-centres or the development and testing of software, could indeed become financially unsustainable in such a volatile economic climate, particularly with fluctuating exchange rates and the uncertainty of related currencies. There may be questions regarding the viability of certain production markets, particularly while Pluto travels through the industry-orientated sign of Capricorn in hard aspect to an unpredictable but innovative Uranus in Aries.

Arguably, the most recent conjunction of Uranus and Pluto in the 1960s has had a larger impact on human history than any other conjunction cycle in the past, as our lives seem to have changed in the last fifty years more rapidly than at any other time in human history. Life has speeded up, and the Uranus–Pluto in Virgo generation likes to be kept busy, either working or doing something else. Here in the UK, we have a Prime Minister and a Deputy Prime Minister (charts opposite and overleaf) who were both born under this conjunction and you will find many of the burning issues of government these days being work, the minimum wage, pension ages, etc., as the Uranus–Pluto squares trigger these areas.

---

62. K. Grint, *The Sociology of Work*, p. 359.

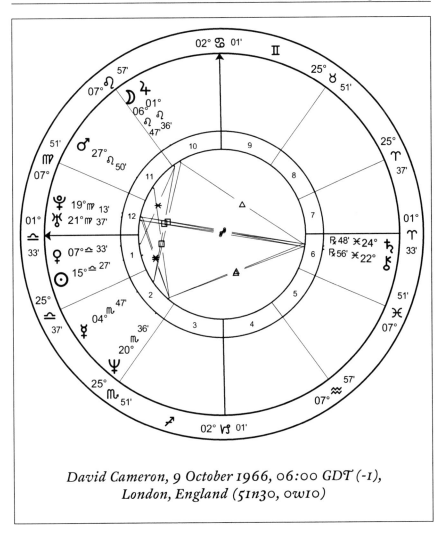

David Cameron, 9 October 1966, 06:00 GDT (-1),
London, England (51n30, 0w10)

In June 2011, 11,000 schools around the UK were closed while teachers protested over pay and pension cuts and the increase in the retirement age.[63] Pensions, although effectively an asset and associated with Taurus, are linked to Virgo because our value is reflected by the work we do and the income we receive. Yet when the economy is crashing and stock markets fall, so do pension pots. With the square of Uranus and Pluto activating the conjunction at the start of the current cycle, working hours, working ages and the benefits that come with

---

63. http://www.bbc.co.uk/news/education-13958932 [accessed 24 March 2012].

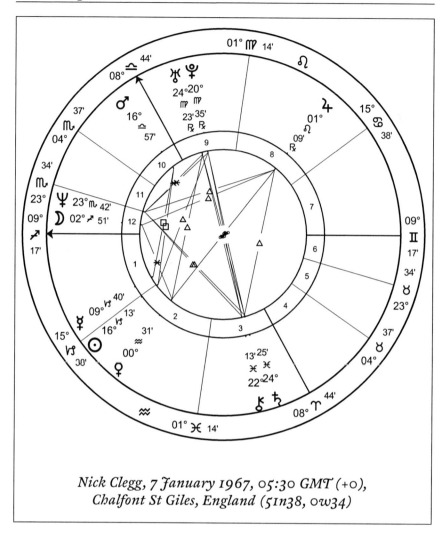

Nick Clegg, 7 January 1967, 05:30 GMT (+0),
Chalfont St Giles, England (51n38, 0w34)

work will be challenged, and these protests, as well as other strike action, are an example of this, as they were in the 60s.

The Uranus–Pluto conjunction generation is work-orientated, and Virgo knows how to work hard; in fact, sometimes it can't resist over-working and sees no problem in raising the retirement age, which will also benefit the state's welfare system, which is also ruled by Virgo. These issues will continue to be in focus while the seven squares of Uranus and Pluto occur over the next few years.

Currently, the unemployment rate in the UK stands at 7.7 per cent,[64] while the US unemployment rate is 9.1 per cent.[65] At the time of writing, countries such as Greece have such a volatile economy that they have an unemployment rate of over 16 per cent.[66] Many of the unemployed in these countries are under the age of twenty-five. Saturn travelled through Virgo from September 2007 to July 2010, which saw the credit crunch and the increase in unemployment. Saturn in Virgo restricts work and inhibits the growth of the labour market around the globe and, since Saturn's most recent transit through this sign, people have been in fear of losing their jobs and have endured income freezes for the sake of job security.

Virgo likes things neat and tidy. The Uranus–Pluto in Virgo generation appreciates stationery and similar items but also has an interest in environmentalism and reducing the use of paper. These are the people who have created the paper-free and minimalist work environment. Our work patterns and working hours have also changed since the 1960s – everything happens round the clock now and for many people there's no stopping work.

Virgo is concerned with process. The sign is well known for being methodical and practical with an eye for detail, so it is no surprise that the Uranus–Pluto generation brought things like CVs, employment contracts and job specifications further into the mainstream. These mechanisms are about ensuring people are doing their job – and properly. They are about being accountable and the segregation of duties, which is incredibly Virgo. This technical generation have been the writers and organizers of sophisticated electronic filing systems, where everything is stored properly.

Virgo likes to pigeonhole things, making them easier to manage and classify. Therefore, working roles and

---

64. http://www.statistics.gov.uk/pdfdir/lmsuk0711.pdf [acc. 24 March 2012].
65. http://www.tradingeconomics.com/united-states/unemployment-rate [accessed 24 March 2012].
66. http://en.wikipedia.org/wiki/Economy_of_Greece [accessed 1 April 2012].

professions have become more defined since the 1960s. Virgo likes projects, and the term 'project manager' has become more popular over the last decade as the Uranus–Pluto in Virgo generation have reached their thirties and forties. The actual project management systems which have been integrated into the corporate and commercial workplace over the last decade are all about organization. Colour-coded spreadsheets which outline every step of any project have now become an essential part of the working day for many. Sometimes organizing this process takes more time than actually doing the tasks laid out in the spreadsheets, but it clarifies the workload and makes the worker more clearly accountable for certain tasks.

Gone are the typing pools, and office space is now redesigned to cater for more people, and everyone has their own cubicle or little space to work in. Neat areas which are organized by dividers are placed throughout offices. The financial implications of having someone occupying desk space is now an integral part of assessing company expenditure (or reducing it), leading to the introduction of the 'hot-desk' environment. With the low cost of remote access, it is now viable (and the financial rewards are measurable) for people to work from home. The more people work from home, the more this will, of course, have an impact on mobilization, property markets and lifestyle.

Virgo wants to help everyone receive fair treatment and the equal employment act or affirmative action policies, whose aims are to avoid discrimination against any person in the workplace, has also become an integral part of company policy. The sign of discrimination (Virgo) wants to ensure that everybody has equal opportunities within the employment sector.

As Virgo is associated with the subject of 'health', the growing issue of 'heath and safety' has become a dominant feature in any working environment. Virgo is associated with defining rules and regulations and assessing risk.

Health

Health practices and policy have radically changed since the 1960s. Virgo rules health and the health of a nation. When Virgo was visited by Uranus and Pluto we saw the growth of medicalization around the globe to unprecedented levels.

The term 'medicalization' refers to an approach to health which gives medical professionals power over the patient – an assumption that 'experts know best'. Medicalization has led to the processing of patients, conveyor-belt style, to follow hospital policies and practices with the aim of increasing profit and/or to ensure efficiency.

Illness and disease, which would have led to debilitation in the past, have become much more treatable, and the majority of people in the developed world now live longer and are more pain-free than ever in human history.[67] We are dependent on the science of medicine, and our attitudes to and expectations of health over the past fifty years have rapidly changed to the point where illness and death are considered untimely, and we are surprised if we encounter illness before old age. We are obsessed with the hygiene of our bodies: recent decades have seen a daily bath or shower for most of us, we brush our teeth at least twice a day, we purify our bodies by subjecting them to a cleaning routine and by attempting to eradicate or treat any viral or bacterial transference. This behaviour, arising from doubt and anxiety about our health, is a social phenomenon, and one that has led to a sense that people are active constructors of their own health.[68]

The traditional first aid box, once located in the bathroom cabinet, has now been extended from the home to the handbag. The bandages, arnica, calamine lotion and iodine now have to be searched for among a flood of compact and

67. Deborah Lupton, *Medicine as Culture*, p. 1.
68. Sarah Nettleton and Jonathan Watson, *The Body in Everyday Life*, p. 121.

mess-free pills such as aspirin (which became popular in the 1960s), Nurofen, paracetamol, antihistamines, cough and flu preventatives, rescue remedies and other little pills or drops for any ailment. The kitchen cabinets in many homes now abound with more antibacterial cleaning products than ever before, and the need to sterilize and purify are key characteristics of the Uranus and Pluto in Virgo generation, to the point where many people carry little bottles of hand-sanitizer wherever they go.

The sign of Virgo rules the digestion, the stomach, the digestive enzymes, spleen, pancreas, diaphragm and the filtering function of the liver. It also rules the sympathetic nervous system.[69] I also think it rules the bowels as part of the digestive function, as well as other health matters such as anxiety and some stress-related headaches. Virgo is the worrying type, which brings anxiety.

Although an Earth sign, Virgo is not only physically inclined; ruled by Mercury, it also seeks mental stimulation, is rational and intellectual and looks for cognitive order as well. It is the sign of analysis. Virgo has a need to regulate, ensuring that everything in the body and mind is doing the right thing at the right time. The areas that Virgo rule have been spotlighted within the last fifty years, most particularly with the increase of eating disorders. These are directly involved with the digestive system and connected to the Virgo maiden, striving for perfection. Eating disorders have probably always been present in society, but have not been as prevalent or as well researched or documented since Uranus conjunct Pluto in Virgo.

Lena Zavaroni, a British child star who was born in 1963, is renowned for winning *Opportunity Knocks* a record-breaking five weeks in a row and for her single, *Ma, He's Making Eyes At Me*. She possessed several Virgo qualities and was someone who strove for perfection when performing. At the

---

69. Jane Ridder-Patrick, *A Handbook of Medical Astrology*.

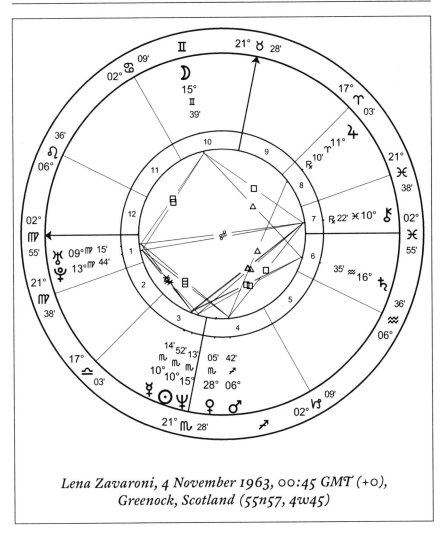

Lena Zavaroni, 4 November 1963, 00:45 GMT (+0),
Greenock, Scotland (55n57, 4w45)

age of thirteen, she was diagnosed with anorexia nervosa
and died at the age of thirty-five from a blood infection while
recovering from a leucotomy (brain operation) to cure her in
September 1999.[70]

Lena Zavaroni was one of the first celebrities to go public
with her anorexia. We understand from her chart (above) that
she has Virgo rising and was born under the Uranus–Pluto
conjunction. These planets are also rising in her chart. The

70. Frank Clifford, *British Entertainers: The Astrological Profiles*, p. 304.

conjunction opposes Chiron and creates a T-square with her Moon (food) in the tenth house. Saturn (placed in the sixth house) and Uranus both rule her sixth house of health. With these strong Virgoan qualities we can see a child who was an incredible perfectionist. The Uranus–Pluto conjunction rising would have felt like huge pressure for her to succeed in her pursuits, and along with the T-square shows an emotional discontentment. Frank Clifford, in his book *British Entertainers: The Astrological Profiles*, documents that she once stated that 'she was unable to cope with an empty feeling she called *static*'.

It could be argued that since the Uranus–Pluto conjunction in Virgo, with the introduction of the 'Twiggy' era, what was deemed attractive in body size started to reshape social demands and, subsequently, a new body politics. People with eating disorders often say that they want to gain control over their bodies.[71] There can also be an element of needing to perfect the body in order to be desirable.

The digestive system is also in focus when we think of the growing obesity problems in the western world since the 1960s. Our relationship with food, and the impact it has on our bodies as well as our mental well being, is continually in focus today. We have become increasingly aware of obsessive-compulsive disorders, and ailments such as Irritable Bowel Syndrome (IBS) have become more widespread in today's society. Virgo is connected with digestion and the body's processing of food, as well as small animals and their welfare, so it is no surprise that when Uranus conjoined Pluto in Virgo in the 1960s, vegetarianism became popular and remains so. In my own experience, I have noticed a lot of people with planets in Virgo (particularly the Moon) who are vegetarian because they feel that their bodies cannot digest meat properly, perhaps also because of a strong instinct to care for animals. Pluto is concerned with death and Uranus is politically driven, so it is not uncommon to find vegetarians

---

71. Deborah Lupton, *Medicine as Culture*, p. 46.

(particularly those with the Moon or other planets in Aquarius) being vegetarian for more political reasons.

Our fear of death, and our obsession with youth and the need to perfect ourselves, creates the need for new technologies in order to postpone the ageing process, as well as to look and feel younger. The emergence of cosmetic surgery since the 1960s is another example of this. Aesthetic beauty has always belonged to the realm of Libra, but Virgo strives for perfection and wants to get things right.

When Uranus and Pluto were conjunct in Virgo in the 1960s, we saw signs of the technological revolution to come and the arrival of a sexual revolution initiated by the invention of the contraceptive pill. From there we have seen a growth in technologies for reproduction, with innovations in childbirth that will change human history in a very short span of time. The Maiden Virgo, as she moves into the stage of motherhood, comes with a new set of rules and systems whereby childbirth and the relationship between mother and body, and mother and child, are changing.

There is much to be learned about this global phenomenon, which appears to be getting out of hand. The Uranus–Pluto generation has a collective need to perfect aspects of society, and birth – along with death – is part of the medicalization process in which efficiency is primary and everything is scheduled, processed and routine to minimize potential risk. The Uranus–Pluto in Virgo generation, with the shadow of Pisces, carries a sense of paranoia and fear of losing control, which is often projected onto the next generation.

The changes in the childbirth process will bring new theories about children and new social pressures and risks that we are not yet fully aware of. Over the last thirty years, medicalization has escalated with the aid of technology, leading to treatments such as IVF, fertility treatment, sperm and egg donor insemination (in the UK, often a trade-off by the NHS for those who cannot afford IVF), surrogacy, scanning machines, foetal monitoring machines, foetal medicine and surgery, an assortment of medication which can be administered for pain relief during labour, hormone stimulants to aid contractions, plus assisted births such as forceps, ventouse and C-sections. We are now able to clone human DNA and will soon be able to perform womb transplants.[72] Prospective mothers are able to terminate pregnancies at up to twenty-four weeks based on unfavourable test results, yet some babies can survive if prematurely born at around twenty-two weeks. This highlights the supposed commitment to avoid discriminating against people with disabilities, with the understanding that they can lead a rewarding life.

It is clear that the attitudes toward birth and child-rearing have changed in recent decades, as has the parenting experience – and there is evidence that this will continue to change, given the technological and time-driven society we live in. The sociologist Barbara Katz Rothman talks about how parents today make radical decisions about their children and raises the point that parents are insistent on controlling the type of child they will be parenting. She writes that the choices are endless and, reminding us of technological progression, she asks: did this start with how the birth should take place, or before, when character traits and abilities (or disabilities) are primary factors for selection? Parents often believe it is their right in their relationship with their child to make such decisions. She asks, 'Do we eventually want to "order them", to have them custom made?'[73] She cautions us to think wisely about the choices we make for our children, and reconsider the choices over which we think we have control. We have opened a gateway to controlled reproduction. In the society we live in today, it would be interesting to know how many people, if offered the choice of having a perfect child, would take it. We need to be reminded that the desire for perfection is a Virgo one.

---

72. R. Smith, 'First Womb Transplants', *Evening Standard*, 4 September 2006, p. 1.
73. Barbara Katz Rothman, *Genetic Maps and Human Imaginations: The Limits of Science in Understanding Who We Are*, p. 211.

Step forward to a dinner party in 2025. Somebody mentions the amount that the Smiths have paid to make sure their next daughter has blue eyes. Wouldn't it have been better spent on making her musical?[74]

There are several feminist debates about whether women really do have control over their bodies – if they really are making informed choices or are being coerced by a male-dominated profession.

In my own PhD research, I conducted a mixed method study. The first part of my study looked at a large data set of when and how babies were born in the last two decades, noting any patterns that have changed, and the second part of my research involved interviewing women to get an understanding of how the childbirth process is experienced today, and to learn why the number of intervened births is increasing and how patterns of the time and day of birth are changing. When I embarked on this research, I expected to find that women were mostly coerced into having Caesarean sections and that they were being processed as quickly as possible by the medical profession. From my interviews with mothers who had given birth by Caesarean section, this was often the case. They used phrases such as 'meat on a slab', and 'conveyer belt', and several used the word 'processed'.

But another narrative became apparent with a lot of the women I interviewed, who made statements such as 'I wanted to know they were doing their job', and 'I wanted to know who was who, and whether they were doing their job properly'. This was interestingly quite common from the mothers born of the Uranus and Pluto in Virgo generation. Many of those who were born in the 1960s seem to be driving this movement, for they like to know or even obsess about ensuring everything is in order, clean and tidy and making sure the right people are at the right station and doing

---

74. Anonymous, 'Editorial', *The Economist*, 14 April 2005, p2.

what they should. This was interesting to hear and perhaps indicates that this situation is not necessarily always about doctors controlling childbirth, but also perhaps about the need for both mothers and health professionals to *organize* childbirth – a Virgo trait.

There is a further problem with the medicalization of childbirth, which is that we cannot know the long-term risks because it is such a new phenomenon. Without medical intervention, it would be reasonable to expect that the distribution of births would occur randomly throughout the twenty-four-hour day. However, although there is limited research available, the distribution of births within a twenty-four-hour period has been found to be historically less random, and time patterns of births are more likely to be grouped into specific parts of the day. This pattern is not dissimilar to studies of the time of death,[75] where people have been found to be more likely to die at certain times of the day (Young, 1988). Research conducted has shown that births are more likely to occur on Sundays and between 3-6 in the morning,[76] possibly because women are more relaxed at this time.

Despite warnings from various global and national health organizations, Caesarean section birth rates in England have increased from 2.7 per cent in 1953 to 11.3 per cent in 1990, 19.2 per cent in 1998, 23.5 per cent in 2006 and 24.6 per cent in 2008. Over 47 per cent of the 2008 birth rates were recorded as being elected Caesarean sections.[77] In 2008, Scotland recorded average rates of 25.8 per cent and Wales 26.1 per cent Caesarean births. Northern Ireland has not recorded birth rates since 2004, when 26 per cent of births were by Caesarean section.

---

75. For example, see Michael Young, *The Metronomic Society*.
76. For example, see Kaiser et al., 'Circadian Periodic Aspects of Birth', *Annals of the New York Academy of Sciences*, pp. 1056-1068; Chamberlain, et al., *British Births 1970*; Macfarlane et al., 'Daily seasonal variation in live births, still-births and infant mortality in England and Wales, 1979-96'. *Health Statistics Quarterly*, pp. 5-15.
77. Birthchoice website, http://www.birthchoiceuk.com/ [accessed 5 July 2009].

This is not just a western phenomenon but one that extends to the many parts of the world where Caesarean births are highly valued and considered elitist and therefore more fashionable. Although the method of delivery is not recorded in parts of India, Madras has now reached annual Caesarean rates of 45 per cent, Shanghai in China has 32 per cent and, in 2001, Brazil recorded a rate of 72 per cent.[78]

In many cases there is a medical need for Caesarean births, as there is for interventions, and these methods should not be ruled out when risk is involved. However, intervention has become a fast-growing trend, even when it is not medically necessary, and high numbers of Caesarean rates have astrological implications.[79] There are also several health professionals who believe we are heading for (or are advocating) a 100 per cent Caesarean-born society.[80]

There are implications for astrology as well as for the wider society, as these intervened births are resulting in babies being born during standard office hours. Due to medical intervention – mainly elective Caesarean sections – a significant number of babies are now being born from Monday to Friday and between the working hours of 9am and 5pm – and the number of these births in our population is increasing at an alarming rate.[81]

This is a recent phenomenon, having started early in the 1990s with the Uranus–Pluto in Virgo generation who were in their thirties at the time. This is the first time in human history that

78. Sheila Kitzenger, *The Politics of Birth*, p. 76.
79. For more information, see my article, Wendy Stacey, 'Pearls of Tomorrow' in *The Astrological Journal*, July/August 2010, pp. 27-34.
80. For example, see: P. Steer, 'Caesarean section: an evolving procedure?', *British Journal of Obstetrics and Gynaecology*, 1998, pp. 1052-5; Kitzenger. *The Politics of Birth*; Sarah-Kate Templeton, 'All Women get right to Caesareans', *The Sunday Times*, 30 October 2011; Thomas Moore, 'Caesarean Births to be allowed on request', *Sky News*, 23 November 2011.
81. Macfarlane, et al., 'Daily seasonal variation in live births, stillbirths and infant mortality in England and Wales, 1979-96', *Health Statistics Quarterly*, 2001, pp. 5-15; Birthchoice website http://www.birthchoiceuk.com/ [accessed 5 July 2009].

young mothers have been both the drivers and the victims of this extraordinary reshaping of the reproductive experience. While we try to perfect our children and organize our preferred method of childbirth, we are creating a selection criteria. If the rise in Caesarean section births becomes so prevalent that there is no longer a need to give birth in the traditional way, then the question begs: Will there be any need to carry babies? If we eliminate the birth process, we might eventually remove the pregnancy experience, too, and if there is no need to be pregnant, will there also be alternative ways to conceive?

The risks of a changing childbirth process in recent decades are as yet unknown. The attempt to improve the survival of newborn babies and their mothers has arguably led to a rise in the control exercised by the medical profession when alleviating any potentially difficult or dangerous outcomes. Yet what we have constructed instead, by trying to replace chance with choice, is the construction not only of a baby industry (from which there is no going back), but also an unknowable future. We have no measure of the risk, if any, that we may have imposed on future generations.

Uranus and Pluto in Virgo brought a new form of contraception in the 1960s in the form of a neat little contraceptive pill. This was liberating for the Maiden and her body. However, since then we have seen new devices and medications that have exponentially spread through the western world, and today, the Maiden can even eradicate the messy issue of menstruation, as most contraceptives have a built-in hormone that stops monthly bleeding. One shadow side of this is the other parts of the world where women have no control over contraception, let alone menstruation, and where they are powerless in the face of health issues such as rising rates of infant mortality, exposure to germs and disease and, in some areas of the globe, the risk of contracting the AIDS virus.

Virgo is also concerned with analysis, and since the 1960s we have seen a growth in the area of self-analysis and psychotherapy. Being the children of the Pluto in Leo generation, the Uranus–Pluto in Virgo generation sought to understand personal psychology and break down the patterns that the previous generation had bestowed. Virgo can be quite critical of Leo and has sought to put right the errors of the previous generation.

Along with a rise in anxiety disorders, there are other ailments connected with stress or exhaustion today which reflect the extremities of Virgo. We will have to look after our bodies in different ways as new ailments and symptoms arise from modern technology, such as mobile phones, becoming an integral part of life.

Virgo needs to break things down. It dissects in order to understand the pattern and mechanism of something. This applies to everything, such as a puzzle or a psychological issue. We are able to perfect silicon chips that replicate the brain by viewing how the brain stores and files information, how our memory works, the parts which enable us to retain sequences of events and digits, letters or words, our electrical impulses, our brain's cellular architecture, and the fine-tuning connections between neurons and memory networks.[82] Metaphorical systems such as this reduce individuals to their DNA codes.

The symbolism of the Uranus–Pluto conjunction in Virgo describes these developments in technology as applied to health – the realm of Virgo. Breaking things down, trying to understand the mechanisms that make the body work, analysing and critiquing, attempting to perfect and fix things, plus objectifying the body and the self, are all key areas that belong to the realm of Virgo and we need to ensure that we do not completely remove ourselves from human experience. It might help to recognize in the first instance that we are well on the path to doing exactly that.

---

82. S. Young and D. Concar, 'These Cells Were Made for Learning', New Scientist Supplement, 21 November 1992.

Industry

When we think of Virgo, one of the main areas that we associate with the sign is work. This extends to all aspects of work, including what we do for a living, how much we earn and the precise nature of our skills, as well as employment on a larger scale. It is interesting to observe industry on a larger scale as well – although also associated with Capricorn, industry will tell us 'what' people do for a living. The Uranus–Pluto conjunction in Virgo had a huge impact on how industry has changed and expanded since that time. This conjunction set the scene for Virgo-related industries to flourish.

Our current society has come to depend upon several industries, but I want to focus here on some of the more dominant ones and those that directly relate to the 1960s Uranus–Pluto conjunction, showing how these will come under the spotlight during the squares between Uranus and Pluto over the next few years. Uranus governs technology, Pluto is the Lord of Wealth, and Virgo is concerned with systems, routine and daily life, so it is no surprise that the technological revolution that began in the 1960s has changed the way billions of people around the globe work.

The invention of the silicon chip and the microprocessor – small compact Virgo components – led to integrated circuit technology, which spearheaded the computer and technological era that we have become so dependent upon. The Information Technology and Global Communications industry has become one of the largest industries in human history, and it continues to expand. The conjunction of Uranus and Pluto marks an interesting era in the development of this industry.

Of course, one of the reasons for its growth is that the human population has, in a very short space of time, become dependent on computers as an integral part of our lives, for work, study and leisure. The growth in this area will continue to expand as this particular astrological period gave birth to a generation of engineers and IT experts who now manage (or hack) various aspects of it and have made it an integral part of their society for the next generation.

We can see Virgo traits entrenched in the way we work with computers and the language associated with it. We protect against *viruses*, we used Virgo words like *on line*, Virgo patterns such as *web*, and we have replaced the craft of handwriting with nice tidy *fonts* to do it for us. We use a mouse and Virgo rules small animals. It is interesting that the Virgo maiden is associated with softness; one could even say *Microsoft*. The forbidden fruit that inveigled virgin Eve to discover her sexuality was an *Apple*. As a wise goddess, one could see Virgo as an *Oracle*. These major and dominating computer companies all carry Virgoan attributes, as do their names!

One particular brand name which has expanded and dominated UK industry over recent decades is the suitably named Virgin; this brand has entered into several industries around the globe. As we know, Virgo is another word for the Virgin. The fact that this name has become so familiar around the world in recent years is indicative of the influence of the sign of Virgo in the present day. The original Virgin logo used in the 1970s was created by English artist Roger Dean (also a Virgo). The logo featured a young woman with a large long-tailed serpent and the word 'Virgin' in the original script. The Virgin logo used today was originally sketched in 1979 on a paper napkin[83] – yet another Virgo-related object!

The brand Virgin, one of the largest in the UK, has now extended its original brand of Virgin Records to a multitude of industries such as Virgin Trains, Virgin Atlantic, Virgin Active, Virgin Mobile, Virgin Media, Virgin Money, Virgin TV, Virgin Radio and, more recently, Virgin Galactic.

---

83. http://www.famouslogos.org/virgin-logo [accessed 21 August 2011].

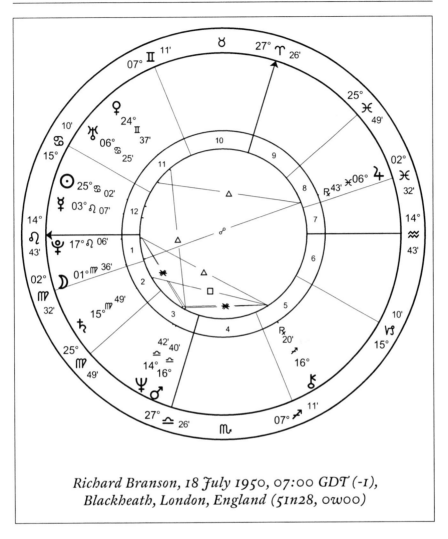

Richard Branson, 18 July 1950, 07:00 GDT (-1),
Blackheath, London, England (51n28, 0w00)

There is another interesting, but not surprising, dimension to the Virgin brand. The man who created this brand is, decades later, still at its helm – Sir Richard Branson.

Branson's chart (above) and we can see from this he was born in 1950. He has a Virgo Moon, which perhaps describes his eye for detail, persistence and the pursuit of perfection. Another most interesting point is that he has Saturn in Virgo at almost 16° – the exact degree of the conjunction of Uranus and Pluto in April and June of 1966. Saturn is an important focal point in this chart; perhaps one of the most dominant features, as it is unaspected. It is not integrated with the rest of the chart as it makes no major aspects to any of the other planets.

When Uranus and Pluto came to conjunction in 1966, Branson entered into his first business enterprise running *The Student*, a successful magazine that promoted music sales. As his business grew and the Virgin label was established, Branson's quick rise to success was largely due to cutting prices and taking on major High Street outlets. He basically created a new competitive edge to the record industry by slashing prices (Uranus–Pluto). This business approach continued and was the foundation of his success in building the Virgin brand and empire. The 1979 Virgin logo that is currently used today was launched on Branson's exact Saturn in Virgo return. Interestingly, when Uranus and Pluto made their first aspect, a sextile between 1995 and 1997 (the first since the conjunction in the 1960s), Branson spent those two years trying to circumnavigate the world by hot-air balloon. The Uranus–Pluto sextile made five exact hits between 27° Capricorn and Scorpio, and between 0, 3 and 5° Aquarius and Sagittarius. Transiting Pluto was square to Branson's natal first house Moon in Virgo and transiting Uranus was square his natal MC.

Virgo rules the digestive system, and there is often a relationship between the world's major industries and what we eat and digest. The generation born in the 1960s has, by their very Uranus–Pluto in Virgo nature, created a demand for healthy foods. Of course there is also a shadow side to this, and here we also see the start of a junk food society. (In the mid-60s the 'M' and Ronald McDonald were added to the then smallish hamburger chain of McDonalds, which is now the largest fast-food chain in the world).

A BBC TV series called *The Food That Makes Billions* was aired in March 2011. This programme tells the story of the three biggest revolutions in functional food industries in the world today – all of them Virgoan! The series sought to illustrate how these food commodities have been scientifically manipulated and marketed to promote health and well being, and how the most versatile of all foods has been transformed into the biggest industries and brands in the world.[84]

The first programme focused on the billion-pound industry of bottled water. It told the story of how populations around the world are dependent on the purification of water. Astrologically, water normally belongs to the three Water signs (Cancer, Scorpio and Pisces), and the containment of water is represented by Scorpio. However, Virgo is connected with the purification of the body and the filtering process. Virgo also advocates cleansing and good health, and the programme brought up some interesting facts about water and dispelled some of the myths, such as people actually not needing to drink eight cups of water a day, and how companies take liberties with the demand for fresh and clean water by not always supplying what they advertise. The scandal involving Coca-Cola's water brand, Dasani, in 2004, was used as an example of tap water being advertised as filtered bottled water.

The second episode addressed the billion-pound cereal industry. It talked about how wheat is in such high demand and how the cereal industry has boomed over recent decades and produced a global breakfast food. The programme also discussed how the beneficial qualities of cereals in no way equate to what is advertised. What is so interesting about this particular industry is that it again relates directly to the Virgo Maiden, who is traditionally symbolized holding sheaves of wheat in her arms. Virgo rules agriculture, grains and the harvest, and is associated with Demeter, the Greek earth goddess who was responsible for regulating the seasons. Here the sheaf of wheat has very literally grown into yet another Virgo industry.

The third and final episode was about yoghurt. Although yoghurt has been around for millennia, it did not gain its

84. http://www.bbc.co.uk/programmes/b00wmvck [accessed 21 August 2011].

popularity in the West until the 1960s, when it began to be promoted as a health food that is rich in nutrition and contains live bacterial cultures that the body needs. The expansion of the yoghurt industry in the past fifty years has owed much of its success to the adaptable nature of yoghurt and the forms in which it can be produced. Virgo is a sign which is mutable, making it highly malleable, and as it rules bacteria it is no surprise that yoghurt products have become a huge global business.

Research, Methods and Data Collection

Another of Virgo's main associations is with research and analysis. Virgo is interested in analysing on every level and for every possible reason, from marketing to scientific research. The number of methodologies and agencies that now exist to conduct research has grown extensively in the past fifty years, advancing what was a relatively small industry into an integral component of every big business and government agency around the globe. The Science Research Council (SRC), now known as the Science Engineering Research Council, was formed in 1965, during the Uranus–Pluto conjunction in Virgo. It was formed with the aim of enquiring into sciences such as astronomy, biotechnology, biological sciences, space research and particle physics.[85]

Because of the demand for research, the sciences have developed significantly in the past fifty years. Virgo is rational and interested in how things work. Uranus is technological and idealistic about the future, and Pluto needs to get to the bottom of things, and when both planets are combined with Virgo they seek to investigate and understand the fundamental mechanics of things.

Numerous other research agencies formed in 1965, exactly during the Uranus–Pluto conjunction, including the Natural Environment Research Council (Virgo is the Earth goddess), the Social Science Research Council (Uranus–Pluto in Virgo is concerned with the analysis of the masses) and the Agricultural Research Council (Virgo rules agriculture).

Additionally, in 1964 the World Medical Association guided medical practitioners in biomedical research which, for the first time, involved human subjects. The organization's task

---

85. http://en.wikipedia.org/wiki/Science_and_Engineering_Research_Council [accessed 21 August 2011].

was to govern all international research ethics and was to define the rules for 'research combined with clinical care' and 'non-therapeutic research'.[86]

Along with these other agencies, astrologers' own astrological data collection started in the mid-60s with Lois Rodden collecting and rating birth data. One of her successors, Sy Scholfield, has 15° Virgo on the Ascendant, conjunct Uranus and Pluto.

Virgo is an Earth sign so therefore has a materialistic quality. Along with the engineering capabilities of Virgo, the sign also rules areas such as manufacturing – the repetitive activities and assembling of components in the production of goods and services. Virgo represents machine work at all levels – where a process is required, Virgo creates it.

Virgo is also sacrificial and interested in helping, so has no problem always going the extra mile when the need arises. The sign therefore also rules the voluntary services.

---

86. http://research.unlv.edu/ORI-HSR/history-ethics.htm [accessed 21 August 2011].

Witchcraft

Virgo has traditionally been associated with craft in all its forms, as well as with magic, ritual and superstition. Witchcraft has stereotypically been associated with women, especially the crone who is often depicted in many children's stories with a large nose and pointed hat.

Denounced by the Bible, for a long time witchcraft had a reputation for being evil and associated with the Devil. That was until the 1960s, when the uprising of the feminist movement and the resurgence of neo-paganism started to embrace the power of the female and the feminine, and (as witchcraft is intrinsically linked with the natural world) the protection of the environment.

Uranus and Pluto are both associated with the occult. Throughout history, whenever these planets aspect each other, the issue of witchcraft comes into focus in society. In 1541, when Uranus and Pluto were in opposition to each other, Henry VIII introduced the Witchcraft Act, which defined witchcraft as a felony – a crime which was punishable by death.

In 1691, a year before the mass hysteria of the witch trials began in Salem, Massachusetts (1692–93), Uranus and Pluto were exactly sextile (and Neptune was travelling through Pisces). Between 1692 and 1693, over 150 people were imprisoned, twenty-nine were convicted, nineteen of whom were executed by hanging, one was crushed to death and more than five died in prison.[87]

Between the five years of 1735–40, Uranus and Pluto remained within a five-degree orb of a sextile. The Witchcraft Act of 1735 saw the repeal of several previous acts. Instead of people being prosecuted on the grounds of witchcraft, they

---

87. http://en.wikipedia.org/wiki/Salem_witch_trials [accessed 21 August 2011].

were now charged for pretending to be witches. In the 1878 Ipswich witchcraft trial, commonly known as the second Salem witch trial (as the court itself was held in Salem), Uranus and Pluto were square to each other. In this case, a fifty-year-old spinster, Lucretia Brown, accused fellow Christian Scientist Daniel Spofford of practising mesmerism and inflicting mind control over people. The case raised a significant amount of media attention and was eventually dismissed by the judge. This was the last witchcraft case to be heard in the US.

Since the 1960s, it has been much more socially acceptable for women to identify themselves as pagans, druids or wiccans. Perhaps with the decline of Christian influence in western societies over recent decades, and with the increased faith in science, witchcraft is taken less seriously by our society and perceived as something harmless or just for fun. We see acceptance of it in popular culture. Since the 1960s we have seen programmes and films which introduced the more 'whiter' side of magic and witchcraft, making it lighter and showing it to be used for the greater good.

In 1964, as the Uranus–Pluto conjunction in Virgo was building, the US television series *Bewitched* began to be aired on television. It ranks as one of fifty greatest TV shows of all time, according to *TV Guide* magazine.[88] This programme is built around a young female witch, Samantha, who struggles with the challenges of being the suburban housewife of a mortal sales executive. Appropriately, Elizabeth Montgomery, the woman who played Samantha – the prim and proper housewife – has Mars, Jupiter and Neptune in Virgo.[89]

In the same year, the musical film *Mary Poppins*, which starred Julie Andrews (who won an Academy Award for Best

---

88. TV Guide magazine, 4 May 2002, at http://en.wikipedia.org/wiki/TV_Guide%27s_50_Greatest_TV_Shows_of_All_Time [accessed 21 August 2011].
89. Elizabeth Montgomery, born 15 April 1933, 16:38 PST, Los Angeles, California, USA. Source: Birth certificate, AA rating.

Actress), was released and became a huge success. The story is of a magical nanny who helps and enthrals children. Her slogan 'practically perfect in every way' sums up beautifully the Virgo quality expressed here. It is of no surprise either that Julie Andrews has Virgo rising as well as Venus and Neptune in Virgo.[90]

In July 1965, three months before the first exact conjunction of Uranus and Pluto in Virgo, J.K. Rowling, author of the Harry Potter series, was born. Rowling's birth time is unknown, so her birth chart (on the page that follows) has been set for midday and the Ascendant set at 0 Aries. Rowling's story of rags to riches is an extraordinary one. She enjoyed writing fantasy books when she was a young child and later graduated from university with a BA in French and Classics. The idea of Harry Potter came in 1990, but writing the book was delayed due to the death of her mother later that year after a long-term battle with multiple sclerosis. Rowling moved to Portugal where she taught English, was married for a short time and had her daughter before returning to the UK as a single mother. She resided in Edinburgh to be close to her sister but was suffering from clinical depression. After her recovery she finished writing the first of the Harry Potter books, *Harry Potter and the Philosopher's Stone*, in 1995. It was rejected by several publishing houses until Bloomsbury agreed to publish it in 1997. To date, Rowling is the biggest selling series author in the world, with sales of over 450 million copies of her books worldwide.

Rowling was born in an era of changing attitudes towards witchcraft. The craft, ruled by Virgo, is prominent in Rowling's chart, not only with the Uranus–Pluto conjunction in the sign, but also with the Moon and Venus in Virgo as well. Additionally, if Rowling was born after 12:23 pm on the day of her birth, Mercury will also be located in Virgo. Rowling's Mercury is unaspected, other than a wide conjunction with

---

90. Julie Andrews, born 1 October 1935, 06:00 BST, Walton on Thames, England. Source: The Clifford Data Compendium quotes a biography, B rating.

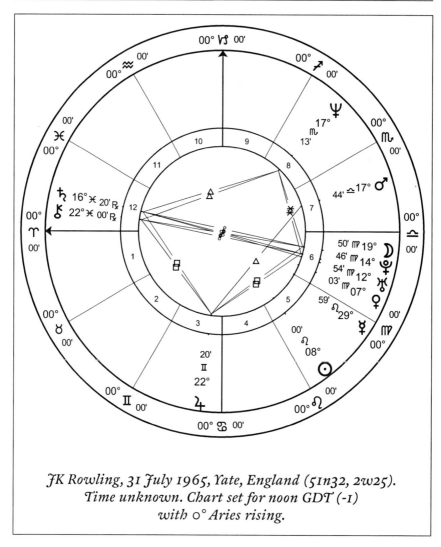

JK Rowling, 31 July 1965, Yate, England (51n32, 2w25).
Time unknown. Chart set for noon GDT (-1)
with 0° Aries rising.

Venus. Her Sun in Leo is also unaspected, and her Venus
only makes a conjunction with Uranus and Pluto, and a wide
conjunction with Mercury. There are strong Virgo elements in
her chart and it is not surprising that Rowling, against all the
odds, became a legendary writer of witchcraft and magic. She
also says that the bookish character of Hermione is one that
she identified with.[91] Perhaps she also identifies with Harry,
as his birthday is revealed as the last day in July, which is also
hers.

91. http://en.wikipedia.org/wiki/J._K._Rowling [accessed 21 August 2011].

The current Uranus–Pluto square is the first time the planets have formed a square aspect since the 1960s conjunction and the birth of Rowling, and is sixteen years after the first Harry Potter book was written. The final film in the series, based on the last book, *Harry Potter and the Deathly Hallows: Part 2*, presented in 3D, was aired at midnight on 15 July 2011, on a full Moon. Uranus was at 4° Aries and Pluto was at 5° Capricorn.

Fashion, Trends and Pop Culture

The pursuit of perfection has become a subconscious aspect of our culture. We still revere the Virgin and there are many examples of this. One, of course, is our own Princess Diana, adored for her innocence, the maiden who stole the hearts of millions around the world. The most photographed woman of all time, revered for her fashion sense and hounded by the paparazzi who intruded on her sexual life. Diana had a dynamic and complex stellium of Mars and Pluto in Virgo widely conjunct Uranus in Leo in the eighth house. She

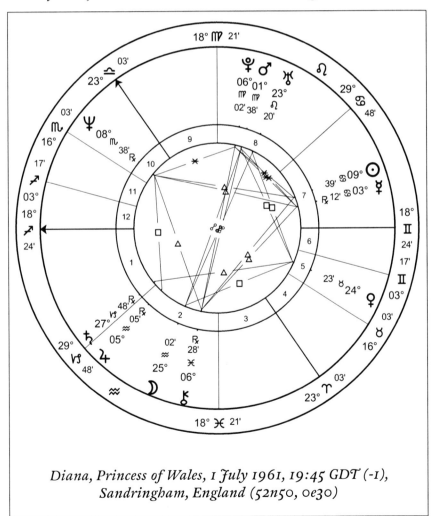

Diana, Princess of Wales, 1 July 1961, 19:45 GDT (-1),
Sandringham, England (52n50, 0e30)

suffered a violent death in 1997 while Uranus and Pluto were separating from a sextile.

Virgo is associated with little and tight things and it is of no surprise that stockings and tights, headbands and miniskirts became fashionable in the 1960s, along with all-in-one outfits such as playsuits and jumpsuits. The 1960s were illuminated by the bright array of short and small things to wear. Fashion trends are interesting to watch: as the planets Uranus and Pluto make their first square to each other after their conjunction in Virgo, these liberating pieces are once more dominating the fashion of today.

Virgo patterns include spots, stripes, squares and checks. Fabrics patterned with black and white symmetrical lines and shapes also appeal to Virgo simplicity. These styles were popular on the front covers of *Vogue* in 1965[92] and are fashionable once again.[93] Fussy, busy but perfectly patterned cloth, another feature of Virgo, yet again returns with the approaching square of Uranus and Pluto.

Hats of all kinds were principal fashion accessories in the 1960s and we can expect to see them return. Hats with bows and flowers, as well as tight, symmetrical and patterned hats, were popular.[94] Virgo rules the sixth house, which represents small and fluffy animals, and we have seen fashion items such as fake fur and animal print fabric becoming popular both then and now.

One of the most famous icons of the 1960s was Twiggy, a British model who was very petite and has had a huge and far-reaching impact on body image ever since. Twiggy was one of the highest paid models of her time and was also known

---

92. http://www.vogue.co.uk/magazine/archive/search/Year/1965 [accessed 24 March 2012].

93. http://www.vogue.co.uk/magazine/archive/issue/2011/January [accessed 24 March 2012].

94. http://www.vogue.co.uk/magazine/archive/search/Year/1969 [accessed 24 March 2012].

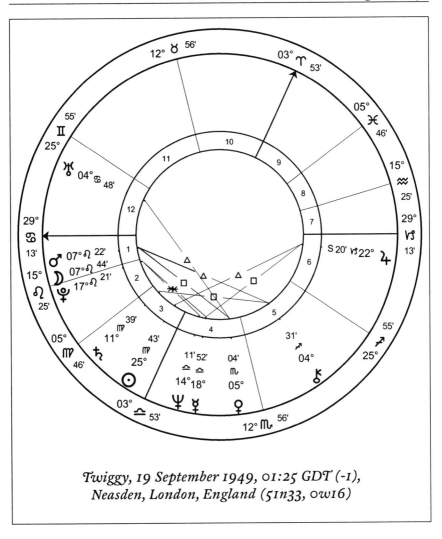

Twiggy, 19 September 1949, 01:25 GDT (-1),
Neasden, London, England (51n33, 0w16)

for her smoky eyes and false eyelashes (which have also come back into fashion recently). Virgo rules the young maiden, which Twiggy so aptly represents, but this girl with the cropped hair also carried with her something new and unique to the fashion industry in the 1960s. This was an androgynous appeal, spotlighting gender politics which underwent major cultural reform during the 1960s, and also bridging the gap between gender identification. Twiggy has both the Sun and Saturn in Virgo.[95] Her bestselling autobiography was called

95. Twiggy, born 19 September 1949, 01:25 BST, London, England. Source:

Twiggy in Black and White and her charity work for animal welfare and anti-fur campaigns are further testament to her Virgo nature.

Other fashion markers from the 1960s were cars. The second most influential automobile of the twentieth century, beaten only by the Ford, was the Mini, which was awarded the title 'Car of the Century' by *Autocar* magazine during the Uranus and Pluto sextile in 1995. The most iconic car of the 1960s,[96] it demonstrated that small, space-saving, versatile and practical features (all Virgo characteristics) could all be given to one vehicle. Films such as *The Italian Job*, released in 1969, both reflected the popularity of the car and helped to increase its sales. The Mini has since had many facelifts and company mergers. During the start of the economic recession in 2008, and the first cardinal climax when Uranus, Pluto and Saturn were forming a T-square, Mini shut down its production for one month. It survived the ordeal and continues to produce the vehicle, which ranked as the seventh biggest selling car in Britain in 2010.[97]

Interestingly, Mini's rival with regards to its compactness and versatility is the Volkswagen Beetle, also popular in the 1960s. It is the longest running and most manufactured car from a single design platform anywhere around the globe.[98] This popular brand was used in the 1968 film *The Love Bug*, which helped to escalate it to its iconic status. These cars mark a period in history where downsizing of automobiles has been useful not just for their convenience and economic value but also for their reduction in petrol emissions.

It is not just what we drive that has spearheaded the demand for small and minimalist living – it is also what we have in our homes. The designs in the most popular furniture outlets

Rectified by Penny Thornton from Twiggy's statement that it was 'in the very early hours of the morning', C rating.

96. http://en.wikipedia.org/wiki/Mini [accessed 24 March 2012].
97. http://en.wikipedia.org/wiki/MINI_(BMW) [accessed 24 March 2012].
98. http://en.wikipedia.org/wiki/Volkswagen_Beetle [accessed 24 March 2012].

reflect the way many people organize their homes. Virgo is mutable and likes everything in its place. Furniture from such outlets as IKEA, with its flat-packed, practical, inexpensive, do-it-yourself ethos and innovative design is conceptually a Virgo creation. The home store Habitat was founded in 1964 by Terence Conran, under the approaching Uranus–Pluto conjunction. On 24 June 2011 (as the Uranus–Pluto square was building) Habitat went into administration and the company was sold off to various purchasers.[99]

The 1960s brought radical reform on many levels and music was a part of this. Popular culture saw revolutionary changes with the unprecedented fame of Elvis and the Beatles (another interesting Virgo name), and mass hysteria as it had never been experienced before. Music became a medium of expression and this was an era where music (and theatre) became political, personal and psychological, and where the audience felt as if they were part of something progressive and were shaking things up. This era saw the widespread use of electric instruments and the breakthrough and popularization of many genres such as heavy rock, folk rock, soul, reggae, Motown and pop. In August 1969, the Woodstock music festival, which over half a million people attended, was possibly one of the most pivotal events in music history and represented a change in social consciousness.

Since then we have seen the Uranus–Pluto conjunction generation introduce other genres such as punk, heavy metal, disco, house, garage and more recently indie and techno. However, with the continuation of the Virgo theme, while this generation has been at the forefront of the music industry, in recent decades we have also seen a lot of repetition in musical trends – another Virgo trait. Major hit songs from decades ago are remade today. In our recycling and lip-syncing culture this is now considered a standard practice in pop music. Our most iconic stars of today seldom perform in public without the security of pre-recorded audio to ensure that the sound is

---

99. http://www.bbc.co.uk/news/business-13901123 [accessed 09 Sept 2011].

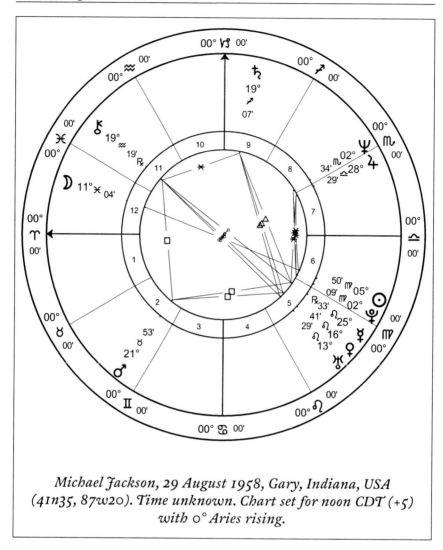

*Michael Jackson, 29 August 1958, Gary, Indiana, USA
(41n35, 87w20). Time unknown. Chart set for noon CDT (+5)
with 0° Aries rising.*

perfect. With the Uranus–Pluto squares we will undoubtedly
see more of a revival of 1960s music and a growing surge
in musical genres that encapsulate the current technological
generation's political and psychological thought.

Icons for the Uranus–Pluto in Virgo generation can be seen
in all corners of society. One that stands out would have to
be the King of Pop. Michael Jackson was born on 29 August
1958. He was originally loved for his innocence as a child star.
As he grew older he became an icon with hits like 'Thriller',
'Beat It', 'Bad' and 'Billie Jean'.

Michael Jackson had the Sun conjunct Pluto in Virgo. He was thought of as someone born before his time. We do not know his birth time and the chart (opposite) has been set for 12 noon with 0° Aries rising. Liz Greene thinks he might have Scorpio rising, which is interesting as it would potentially place his Sun–Pluto in Virgo around the Midheaven. He was a perfectionist, being involved in all of his productions in every step of the way. His sexuality was even addressed in an interview with Oprah Winfrey in 1993 when she inappropriately asked him if he was a virgin, to which he replied, 'I am a gentleman'. Later in his life, his sexuality came under the spotlight again with allegations of child molestation that devastated his career.

However, for decades we watched him destroy himself as he obsessed over what he thought was physical perfection and frequently went under the knife. He was a hypochondriac and, although a health fanatic, was an avid user of pharmaceuticals – his Pisces Moon and other points in his chart contribute to these areas in his life as well. But the King of Pop, with his Sun conjunct Pluto in Virgo, had a huge impact on music, video and dance for the Uranus–Pluto generation.

Another music icon revered by the Uranus–Pluto generation is, of course, the Queen of Pop, Madonna (chart overleaf), born on 16 August 1958, only thirteen days before Jackson. They both have planets in Leo, which would have elevated them to their royal titles (although from the first section in this book, Martin Luther King and Rodney King also possess royal names without Leo planets) but here the perfectionist is again illustrated by her Virgo characteristics. Madonna has the Moon in Virgo conjunct her Virgo Ascendant, and also Mercury and Pluto in Virgo.

Besides the fact that her name is associated with the most famous virgin of all time, what is also interesting about Madonna is that one of her earliest singles (and first US Number One) was 'Like a Virgin' and one of her albums was called *The Immaculate Collection*. Her sexuality also

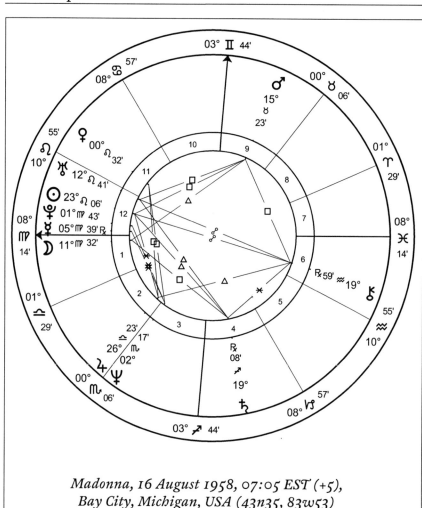

Madonna, 16 August 1958, 07:05 EST (+5),
Bay City, Michigan, USA (43n35, 83w53)

came under the radar as her music and sexual expression developed to such a point that she was criticized by the Catholic Church.

Both the King and Queen of Pop, born less than two weeks apart, were renowned firstly for their virginal and then their explicit sexual behaviour on and off stage. Both rebelled against their religious upbringing and fed the Uranus–Pluto generation with their sexual empowerment and ability to continually reinvent themselves.

Pop art became another trend in the 1960s. This ironic and satirical type of art was already on its way to becoming popular in the 1950s, but Andy Warhol had a huge influence in bringing this form of abstract expressionism to the forefront of 1960s society. What is interesting with regards to Virgo and its characteristics is that Warhol's work was renowned for its repetition of images and everyday things like Campbell's soup. Warhol's painting, 'Eight Elvises', was sold for $100 million in 2009. Several other paintings, in particular those featuring the image of Marilyn Monroe, also display the symmetrical and repetitive patterns in his work. He also introduced the psychedelic painting style, which was so popular in this decade.

Warhol's work will be once again exhibited during 2012 in London and brought to the attention of the world as it is displayed throughout the Olympic Games.

It is interesting to compare this type of art with what is popular today. We are once again in a period where painting pushes the boundaries of what constitutes art, making some contemporary artists as controversial as Warhol was in his day. Living in a growing technological era has also spearheaded imaging technologies, and with the ingress of Neptune into Pisces we might see an increase in the use of computers in artwork in the next decade.

Since the conjunction of Uranus and Pluto in Virgo in the 1960s we have seen human craftsmanship and expression radically change in the arts, leisure and hobby industries. With our progression into the digital age, crafts such as tapestry, sewing and jigsaw puzzles have declined. As astrologer Bernard Eccles once said at a Sophia Centre conference in 2006, the calculation by hand of the natal chart is now akin to old knitting patterns.[100] Instead, the Uranus–Pluto conjunction in Virgo generation has largely replaced much of our traditional crafts with electronic devices for which

---

100. Bernard Eccles, Sophia Centre Conference, Bath Spa University, 2006.

we do not know the physical and psychological effects. However, in saying this, we can expect to see a resurgence of traditional crafts during the Uranus–Pluto squares.

Other Current Planetary Cycles

As astrologers we understand that cycles do not operate in isolation. At any given point, there are cycles within cycles and all these need to be put into perspective against the backdrop of the larger planetary cycles.

For instance, the largest cycle currently known in our solar system is that of the two outermost planets, Neptune and Pluto. The last time these planets came into conjunction was in 1891 and 1892, firstly at 8° and then at 7° Gemini. The conjunction marked the start of this cycle and set the scene for the following 492 years, so any cycle that occurs during this period needs to be considered within the context of this larger cycle. For example, in the relatively short space of time since the 1891 Neptune–Pluto conjunction in Gemini we have seen unprecedented major historical developments in travel, transportation, communications and networks. Planes, automobiles and advancements in roads and public transport have become a way of life, enabling humans to be mobile in ways never before experienced. Communications such as telephones, and later the Internet, are key markers in history, as is the way we communicate through social networking. According to the BBC, YouTube now has 2.9 billion users,[101] and is now a common means for self- or mass-promotion (Justin Bieber is a good example of this). The traditional ways of getting information – by going to libraries and looking things up in books – have changed, with libraries closing due to the Internet and access to resources such as Wikipedia. We are surrounded by devices that communicate to us from portable computers and mobile phones, as well as radio and TV, and society is monitored through CCTV on a national level and satellites on a global one. We are living

---

101. *BBC News*, 19 November 2011.

through an 'information' age, all of which can be attributed to the greatest outer planetary cycle of Neptune and Pluto which conjoined in the sign of Gemini: the traits associated with this sign are reflective of the deep cultural changes that have taken place. One of our biggest worries with an information age is that we need to learn how to filter the junk from the relevant, valid and valuable information, as well as finding a way to filter the information that reaches our children – an increasing concern that will continue to be addressed by our politicians and legal systems.

In the last few years, as we have been building up to the global crisis, several planets have made challenging aspects to each other and we have seen the ingress of all the outer planets into cardinal signs, except for Neptune and Chiron which have made ingresses into mutable Pisces. We have witnessed the long mutual reception between Uranus and Neptune, which has recently come to an end. It is helpful to consider these other planets and their aspect cycles to help us understand the wider context of the Uranus–Pluto cycle and recent events.

The Jupiter–Saturn Cycle

Charles Harvey considered Jupiter and Saturn to be the great chronocrators (or markers of time). It is their cycle that represents great changes in history, and he writes, 'their cycle can be considered the ground base of human development which marks the interaction between the perception of ideas, potentialities, possibilities (Jupiter) and their manifestation in the concrete material world (Saturn)...'[102]

When Jupiter and Saturn conjunct each other in the sky every twenty years we experience changes in our society and at an individual level which have a marked effect on human history. Although these planets operate within the backdrop of the outer planets and their cycles, they orchestrate changes in our social structures, government and all its branches and agencies, legal and financial systems, and they also regulate our social order. They are the rulers of policy and legislation and their astrological positioning will reflect the economies of markets and industries. They tell us about fashion and our ideology; our social beliefs, attitudes, opinions and practices of the time. The cycles of these planets are indicators of how we live with each other, identify and express ourselves socially and nationally.

On 28 May 2000, Jupiter and Saturn made their twenty-year conjunction at 22° Taurus. With the bull as their focus it was no surprise that, following this conjunction, the UK economy was crippled. Foot and mouth and bovine spongiform encephalopathy (BSE, popularly called 'mad-cow' disease), two diseases that affect cattle, were concerns for many years. We also entered into a war involving one of the world's most sought-after resources at present – oil – sixteen months later, and this is still continuing.

---

102. Charles Harvey, *Mundane Astrology*, p. 184.

Taurus is ruled by the planet Venus and associated with love, money and security. However, the conjunction was also in a line-up of planets in Taurus (in the first week of May 2000, the Sun, Moon, Mercury, Venus and Mars were also in Taurus) and the conjunction of Jupiter and Saturn was making a square to Uranus in Aquarius, a sign that rules technology. Five months earlier, the world had been anxiously crossing its collective fingers, hoping that the millennium and century date change wouldn't throw the electronic world into chaos; fortunately, this never occurred. However, on 10 March 2000, when Jupiter and Saturn were applying to conjunct, the Dot-com crisis shook the economy around the world by sending IT markets toppling. Additionally, on 4 May, with Jupiter and Saturn applying to conjunct in the sky (along with the Sun, Moon, Mercury and Venus, all square to Uranus), the first major Internet virus, named 'The Love Bug' or 'ILOVEYOU', was released. It infected 50 million PC users globally at a cost of US $5.5 billion.

In 1980, Jupiter and Saturn made their first conjunction in the element of Air (Libra), but will not remain continuously in this element until their *mutation conjunction* on 21 December 2020 when they conjoin at 0° Aquarius.

When Jupiter and Saturn begin their unbroken sequence of conjunctions in the Air element they will undoubtedly shift human focus from 'ownership' and 'material resources', represented by the Earth element, to a more mental one where 'intellectual property' and the 'sharing of resources', along with speedy and diverse exchange of information, ideas and the ability to move around by efficient travel innovations that will carry us around the planet (and outside it), will occupy the forefront of our economy and dominate our lives.

As mentioned above, this cycle will operate against the backdrop of the Neptune–Pluto conjunction in Gemini of 1890–91, as well as the Mercury-ruled conjunction of Uranus–Pluto in Virgo in 1965–66. This may suggest a shift in focus for the next generation: our grandchildren might not be interested in mortgages or owning their own homes, nor in waging wars over natural resources. They are likely to be a very different generation to us, attracted more by pushing the boundaries in technology and information and focusing on innovations that provide stimuli, not security, and the assimilation and integration of these principles in their lives. There will probably be a change in perception and people will identify themselves with what they know, not with what they own.

We can already glimpse the shift between Earth and Air as we live through a technological revolution that provides and meets the demand for quick fixes and instant gratification, with instant access to global networks and countries. We have seen shifts in working practices as technology has allowed for more mobility, with paper-free and subsequent 'hot-desk' environments in offices. Similarly, the retail industry has had to survive by moving some of its business from high street shops to online shopping, competing with Internet shopping, libraries have fewer visitors as people can access information through a multitude of virtual libraries on the Internet, and so on.

The last time that Jupiter and Saturn began their journey of conjunctions through the Air element was 1226 and the conjunctions remained in this element until 1405 (although they did conjunct in the next element in the sign of Scorpio in 1306 and 1365). This was the High Middle Ages, which saw warmer climates and famine throughout Europe due to an increase in population, not too dissimilar to the issues of the present day.

We have recently (in 2010 and 2011) experienced a series of oppositions between Jupiter and Saturn – their half-cycle – which has added to the world's conflict and social unrest. The oppositions occurred on the following dates:

> 23 May 2010   27° Pisces (Jupiter) and Virgo (Saturn)
> 16 August 2010 2° Aries (Jupiter) and Libra (Saturn)
> 28 March 2011   14° Aries (Jupiter) and Libra (Saturn)

In 1951, when the first Jupiter–Saturn opposition in a sequence of three was at 27° Pisces–Virgo followed by one at 14° Aries–Libra in 1952, Britain saw Winston Churchill return to leadership on 26 October 1951 after a general election and an almost hung parliament. The Tories surprisingly formed the next Parliament with a small majority and with the help of the National Liberals, exactly as it happened after the general election on 6 May 2010!

Other issues around the globe were taking place during the opposition of these planets in 1951. These included crisis talks between the UK and Iran, Korea and Egypt. We saw the South African government's decision to remove black people's votes from the electoral register (14 May 1951).[103] The USA and USSR were testing atomic bombs, while we in the UK were developing our own, despite expressing our opposition to them. And another event in Britain saw the largest peacetime oil fire, as 12 million gallons of petrol blazed at the Avonmouth Docks (6 September 1951).[104]

During the recent opposition phase across the same signs, we have not only seen a massive oil spill and terrible environmental disaster – the Deepwater Horizon oil spill in the Gulf of Mexico between April and July 2010 – but also fires in London during the riots of August 2011, both involving water and fire as the oppositions move from Water-Earth to Fire-Air. Jupiter and Saturn are not usually associated with events such as these, certainly not in isolation; however, what they do represent are social problems, social conscience, social responsibility and social change, and these events very much included these elements.

---

103. *Chronicle of the 20th Century*, p. 717.
104. *Chronicle of the 20th Century*, p. 722.

It should be noted that although two out of three of the 2010–11 oppositions of Jupiter and Saturn occurred at the same degrees as those of 1951–52, and we can expect similar themes to occur, the current situation is different and aspects from other planets to Jupiter and Saturn are different to those in the early 1950s with other different planetary positions. For example, while Uranus was involved in the opposition by forming a T-square to it in 1952, in 2010 and 2011 we find Uranus making a conjunction to Jupiter and an opposition to Saturn, as well as an exact square to Pluto (on 16 August 2010), creating a T-square between all these planets. Thus the Jupiter–Saturn opposition has been tied in with the Uranus–Pluto square of recent years, and the combination has had more far-reaching effects than one would normally expect from a Jupiter–Saturn opposition.

With the mutation into Air, we are at some odds as to what to expect, as everyday life has changed significantly over the past eight centuries and it is difficult to compare one period with another. What we can foresee is that Jupiter–Saturn, both in its conjunctions and oppositions, will mark conflict and changes in society's infrastructure, and as drivers of the economy we can expect that aspects of it with which we have become familiar will either change or go into a state of flux as we enter a new elemental cycle between the planets from 2020.

The Jupiter–Uranus Cycle

When these planets come together they can be guaranteed to bring an element of surprise, sudden awareness and unpredictability, and it can be quite manic. In conjunction they are exciting, maverick and optimistic; however, they can also drop to the bottom as quickly as they can rocket skywards, so their influence on the mood of society can feel like a rollercoaster.

Jupiter and Uranus represent thunder and lightning, and they give rise to anticipation, a sense of restlessness or unease about not knowing what is to come, which can be exhilarating but also scary. When these two planets come together they challenge and disrupt, and will break down stale aspects of the status quo to make way for new opportunities and innovations. Each of them is known for being controversial and together they are 'provokers'.

Before the 1997 Jupiter–Uranus conjunction we lived in quite a different world in which children knew nothing about SMS, MSN, Facebook or Twitter. The skills needed to use these tools have had to be learned by most of us, but for the younger generations they are merely a matter of course. We enter a new age, not knowing what it will bring, but having some idea that technological innovations will change our lives rapidly, as they have done in the past few decades.

Before 1997, the mobile phone was considered by many to be a luxury item with very little value in everyday life, business or otherwise. Although e-mail and the Internet existed, the vast majority of the population did not have e-mail or electronic file sharing, nor any concept of the World Wide Web, let alone Amazon, Ebay, PayPal or Wikipedia.

In hindsight, we are amazed by the misjudgement of quotes such as these:

I think there is a world market for maybe five
computers.
                    Thomas Watson, Chairman of IBM, 1943

There is no reason anyone would want a computer in
their home.
                    Ken Olson, President, Chairman and founder of
                              Digital Equipment Corp, 1977

640K ought to be enough for anybody.
                                         Bill Gates, 1981

On 16 February 1997 Jupiter and Uranus were conjunct in
Aquarius for the first time in this sign in 83 years. By the
end of 1997, many people had started using personal mobile
phones, got themselves an e-mail address and begun to use
the World Wide Web, all of which many would find it difficult
to live without today. By December 1997, Hotmail, the new
free e-mail provider, had 8.5 million registered users.

Of course the mobile phone, personal computer and the
Internet were all invented before the 1997 Jupiter–Uranus
conjunction in Aquarius, but this conjunction introduced us
to a new 'era' which spearheaded the unprecedented and
irreversible evolution of global telecommunications and
electronic devices around the world, which (along with the
ingress of Pluto into Sagittarius in 1995, and the Uranus-
Neptune conjunction in 1993) have been largely responsible
for the globalization process that ensued.

August 1997 saw the re-release of Windows 95 – version 4
(or OSR2.5 version) which included easy browser options,
as well as Internet Explorer 4 which gave user-friendly web
access and saw new enterprise within the telecommunications
and electronics industry. This included the introduction of
competing Internet service providers, operating systems,
advancements in hardware and software, hand-held game
devices and working tools such as Game Boys and PDAs, the
expansion of cable television and home gaming systems, and

the increase in satellite systems, and led to innovations such as broadband and fibre optic cabling. These new tools spun us into a technological age that was inconceivable even only a decade before.

Jupiter and Uranus come together by conjunction approximately every fourteen years and we have experienced a series of their conjunctions in recent years:

8 June 2010	0° Aries
19 September 2010	28° Pisces
4 January 2011	27° Pisces

These conjunctions saw them enter Aries and then go back into Pisces. In Aries we can gather that they will offer something new, give birth to innovations and enterprises we have not seen before, but as they retreat back into Pisces we can also expect these initiatives to be somewhat hidden. Their retreat from Aries to Pisces can also indicate the mass assimilation of something quite fresh and pioneering. As they ingress into the cardinal signs they will undoubtedly bring about massive change around the globe and stimulate technological advancement, particularly within the context of the wider Uranus–Pluto cycle, which is about the reform of innovation and technology.

It is important to note that this conjunction, which occurred three times over 2010 and 2011, is part of a T-square formed by an opposition to Saturn in Libra and a square to Pluto in Capricorn. This will have some bearing on how the Jupiter–Uranus conjunction is expressed. Saturn is grounding and brings concrete reality, structure and productivity, but it is heavy, pessimistic, divides, censors and creates hurdles. In opposition, Saturn's pragmatism is in direct conflict with the insight and foresight of the Jupiter–Uranus conjunction, and from this we can expect to see conflict on many levels.

Like Saturn, Pluto brings dread. With all these major planets in hard aspect to each other, and as they all ingress into cardinal signs, there will be conflict and subsequently an increased anxiety and sense of insecurity and the need for protection around the world. There will be battles fought on many levels. Presently, we are in the midst of wars on the ground, economic wars and ideological wars, as well as a series of natural disasters building up to this major T-square.

British soldiers are still fighting in Afghanistan and Iraq, although there is little coverage of this in the news, and I imagine that if you surveyed children in high schools most of them would not believe it. This is an economic war masked by ideological arguments, and the Jupiter–Uranus conjunction will spotlight this. Perhaps because of its aspects to Saturn and Pluto, this conjunction also paves the way for innovative weapons to be created as we shift from a soldier-based military to a cyber force, and where traditional fighting in airspace and on battlefields will now be reassigned to the attack and defence of competing cyber infiltration technology.

On 19 October 2010, Prime Minister David Cameron announced the government would be making cuts to the British Armed Forces that would result in the loss of 42,000 jobs over the next five years. Caroline Wyatt reported on the BBC evening news on the same day:

> Britain's forces are to shrink and their budgets too, but not the UK's ambitions to be a global player... In terms of the budget, the UK still remains a global player, spending 37 billion a year on defence... The UK is the fourth biggest military spender in the world next to the US, China and France... so getting rid of tanks and Cold War kit makes sense, and more money will be spent on boosting cyber defence and special forces, both contributions valued by our NATO allies, in an information age with new battlegrounds... In the future there will be more emphasis on preventing wars, with the Armed Forces being used only as a last resort.[105]

---

105. Report by Caroline Wyatt, *BBC News*, 19 October 2010.

The Jupiter–Uranus conjunction in Aries and Pisces will give rise to a new era of developing and producing technology at an exceptional depth and pace. Unfortunately we live in a society in which improving the quality of military software will be a priority and also a determinant of how and where we are positioned on global warfare.

An example of this is detailed in two articles published in *The Economist* in September 2010 that relate to Stuxnet, a new cyber weapon that has been described as 'amazing, groundbreaking and impressive'. This new software is a worm with the ability to infiltrate and disrupt 'the operation of a particular process or plant', which has included a nuclear plant in Iran. It has the ability to disable a country's power grid and cyber infrastructures.

On 19 June 2011, on page 3 of *The Sunday Times*, Tony Blair announced that he's worried that solar flares will bring down the UK's entire national grid. There was a large illustration of what solar flares could do. This was strangely timely given the exposure of worm software that also threatens our national grid.

At the present time we are faced with global economic problems that, as yet, seem impossible to resolve. It is important to note that the last time Jupiter–Uranus conjoined at 0° Aries was on 25 January 1928, and Jupiter then squared Pluto on 31 March. As we know, this was a highly volatile period economically, and the stock market crashed on 29 October 1929. Today, we have unprecedented debts that can no longer be ignored in the western world, while China is buying up foreign debt and doesn't know where to invest its reserves. Banks are optimistic (Jupiter–Uranus) and have introduced quantitative easing which allows them basically to write blank cheques to increase their reserves and re-invest funds they do not have. At the same time, the Basel Committee has introduced Basel III, which requires banks to have a long-term plan for heavier regulation and to increase reserves to eliminate risk and absorb shocks (Saturn).

Jupiter–Uranus conjunctions can also be associated with volcanic eruptions and earthquakes, as they tend to shake things up. With Saturn opposing and Pluto in Capricorn squaring these planets, land and the earth will be a factor. Although unfortunate, it is no surprise that there were several horrendous earthquakes over this period of conjunctions, starting in 2010 with Haiti, Chile and Mexico.

The volcanic eruptions that began in Iceland on 21 March created such a thick cloud of ash that air travel around Europe was disrupted for many weeks. The earthquakes killed hundreds of thousands of people and the volcanic ash cloud had a huge impact on the global economy. Astrologer Robin Ray, in the summer 2010 UK APAI Newsletter, writes about the volcanic ash and the astrological configurations at the time, and notes the vulnerability of the angles and planets on the early degrees of the cardinal axis in Iceland's national chart.

Large and devastating earthquakes occurred in Christchurch, New Zealand (4 September 2010 and again on 22 February 2011) and the earthquake followed by a tsunami in Japan (11 March 2011). Residents of Christchurch had been warned that they were due a substantial earthquake in the region; however, what makes these Christchurch earthquakes particularly interesting with regard to the Jupiter–Uranus conjunction is that these planets are connected with discovery and expansion, and the first earthquake (which measured 7.1 on the Richter scale) was only 11km deep and was on a fault line that no one had known existed! It is also worth noting that New Zealand's dominion chart (26 September 1907, 00:00 OZT, Wellington) has the Sun, Venus and MC/IC axis between 1° and 5° of cardinal signs.

When Jupiter and Uranus come together they bring into the collective consciousness questions about truth and freedom, and the need to seek emancipation or liberation on some level. When these planets are conjunct we often see the fight for democracy and human rights. In 1968, in the build-up to the Jupiter–Uranus conjunction (which was in a wide conjunction with Pluto), both Martin Luther King and Robert Kennedy, two individuals associated with the human rights movement in the USA, were assassinated. The Vietnam war was unpopular and there were mass protests on the streets. In the present day we see many people around the globe fighting for democracy and freedom, and there may be further conflict in defence of their human rights. Also interesting is that the Nobel Peace Prize in 2010 was awarded to imprisoned Chinese dissident Liu Xiaobo, which will no doubt create friction with the Chinese government.

When Jupiter and Uranus conjunct there is a desire to unite. People get together to 'make a stand'. There is a desire for a shared ideology, a common belief system, and these planets can be quite ruthless when making their statement. With Saturn opposing and Pluto squaring the current Jupiter–Uranus conjunction, there will be more challenges ahead for the collective.

We can also expect innovation. For example, during the Jupiter–Uranus conjunctions of 1969 we saw some of the most pivotal innovations in air and space travel to date. On 2 March 1969, Concorde, the Anglo-French supersonic airliner, made its first maiden flight. On 21 July 1969, the day after the last in that series of conjunctions, man first set foot on the Moon. This achievement had an incredible impact of the mood and aspirations of the people of the world.

In late March 2010, as Jupiter and Uranus were building to their first conjunction, we saw the successful testing of the hypersonic rocket, an aircraft which can travel over five times faster than the speed of sound. This craft will be able to fly travellers from Heathrow to Sydney in under two hours (which will undoubtedly affect the price of land around the globe, as people will be able to commute to work in other countries more easily). Later that same year, on 10 October 2010, Virgin Galactic successfully launched its first solo flight for its suborbital spacecraft, *Enterprise*. It successfully glided from 45,000 feet for 11 minutes before landing. The next day President Obama authorized and encouraged NASA to progress in human space flight.[106]

While Jupiter and Uranus together can provoke and be incredibly ruthless, they can also bring insight and foresight for a new era, which is quite exciting to a world facing such hard and challenging times.

106. Satoshi Kambayashi, 'Fumbling Towards a Truce', *The Economist*, 14 October 2010).

The Jupiter–Pluto Cycle

Jupiter and Pluto come together by conjunction every twelve years. Broadly speaking, Jupiter enlarges the Pluto principle, and Pluto destroys Jupiterian principles. This planetary cycle brings with it religious change and the exposure of rotten and corrupt beliefs in our society. It also brings inflation, over-confidence or seeking the truth about the current economic situation. It can swing between excessive optimism and extreme pessimism. An increase in knowledge and seeking those out who abuse power will also be highlighted during this period.

The most recent conjunction became exact only once, on 11 December 2007, at 28° Sagittarius. The last time these planets were conjunct at 28° Sagittarius was in 1023 which was an incredibly interesting time for England, and the period leading up to the famous Battle of Hastings and Norman Conquest of England in 1066 (the UK 1066 chart has the Moon at 29° Pisces, Uranus at 28° Sagittarius and Chiron at 26° Virgo, Jupiter and Saturn were also in Virgo) so we may assume that this is a significant conjunction for the UK and note the degree and sign position for future events. Charles Harvey makes interesting reference to the late mutable degrees of the zodiac corresponding to British history and monarchs.[107]

In 2008, Jupiter at 8° Capricorn was separating from its conjunction to Pluto, which had now also entered Capricorn. Jupiter and Pluto can be seen to play a major part in highlighting the global debt problem and financial meltdown around the globe. This period brought the end of the credit culture, and this conjunction along with Pluto entering Capricorn led to the 'credit crunch', as we have come to call it. The Jupiter–Pluto cycle also breeds fear and mass paranoia. We have gone from a period where anything was possible

---

107. Michael Baigent, Nicholas Campion and Charles Harvey, *Mundane Astrology*, p. 328.

in a positive sense to now living through a period where anything is possible in a negative sense. This will continue as Pluto travels through the pessimistic and cautious sign of Capricorn. Anxiety will continue because people don't know what to expect any more – their financial security blanket, provided by institutions such as the banks, the government, employment and pensions companies, is now heavily under threat.

Global safety is brought into question under this cycle as well. The use of the Internet has expanded freedom of information, but it has also extended the scope for surveillance and, with the mass usage of social networks such as Facebook, has also invaded our privacy as never before.

The Saturn–Uranus Cycle

The Saturn–Uranus cycle takes forty-five years to make one revolution. This cycle is concerned with breaking down existing structures, particularly national and government ones, and re-establishing them. Saturn–Uranus also likes to derail and decentralize aspects of society. It is renowned for marking periods of economic crisis as well as intellectual and scientific developments.

The last conjunctions of Saturn and Uranus occurred in 1988 on the following dates:

13 February 1988	29° Sagittarius
26 June 1988	28° Sagittarius
18 October 1988	27° Sagittarius

In 1989 we saw the breakdown of the Berlin Wall. Saturn represents bricks and mortar, and rebellious Uranus smashes and brings things down. In the UK we had the property market crash (1989) and also experienced a mini stock market crash around the world which in particular hit the American Dow Jones (Black Monday on 19 October 1987). The Cold War was finally coming to an end; the Soviet Union was at war with Afghanistan; IRA bombings were occurring in the UK; the US was building up to the Gulf War; and global economic restructuring followed all these events. It was the breakdown of the Soviet Union's economic system that made America *the* superpower, which had a huge effect on the rest of the world.

The oppositions occurred more recently, on the following dates:

4 Nov 2008	18° Virgo (Saturn) and Pisces (Uranus)
5 Feb 2009	20° Virgo (Saturn) and Pisces (Uranus)
15 Sept 2009	24° Virgo (Saturn) and Pisces (Uranus)
27 April 2010	28° Virgo (Saturn) and Pisces (Uranus)
26 July 2010	0° Libra (Saturn) and Aries (Uranus)

Often during the opposition period there is a restructuring of government institutions and election procedures. Between 2010 and 2011 we have been witnessing the revolts and protests around the world, particularly in North Africa and the Middle East. Saturn–Uranus can be violent and show little tolerance. It takes very few prisoners.

The Saturn–Pluto Cycle

The Saturn–Pluto cycle lasts for between thirty-two and thirty-six years. The current cycle began on 8 November 1982, when the planets conjoined at 27° Libra. The next conjunction will be in 2020, when they conjunct at 22° Capricorn.

Saturn and Pluto are very much concerned with control and power, as well as materialism. When these planets make hard aspects to each other (by way of conjunction, opposition or square), economic doom and gloom presides. They can indicate violent events, highlight deprivation on every level, lead to major conflict over power relations and bring forth large-scale population control through audit and surveillance.

During the build-up to their conjunction in 1982, the UK was involved in the Falklands War (April–June), which was predominantly concerned with land (Saturn) and power (Pluto). Also in the Middle East, although conflict had existed for some time beforehand, we saw the first Lebanon War with the attempt by the Israelis to break down the growing power and infrastructure of the Palestine Liberation Organization (PLO).

One of the most historically defining moments of mass murder, which led to several of the wars and conflicts of recent times, took place on 11 September 2001 (now known as '9/11'). This was a coordinated set of four terrorist attacks on the Twin Towers of the World Trade Center in New York, and the Pentagon in Arlington, Virginia, attributed to al-Qaeda. Nearly 3,000 civilians died in the attacks, and this led to the infamous 'War on Terror' that triggered wars between the USA, and its allies, and Afghanistan and Iraq. The 9/11 attacks occurred shortly after a Saturn–Pluto opposition at 12° Gemini–Sagittarius. This opposition exactly straddles the Ascendant/Descendant axis of the US Sibly chart. The imagery of the event ties in with the Gemini/Sagittarius axis, as the attacks involved aviation (ruled by both signs) and the 'Twin' towers (Gemini) were targeted. Not long after the next series of hard aspects (the squares between Saturn and Pluto), Osama bin Laden, the man held responsible for masterminding the attacks, was shot and killed on 2 May 2011.

In April 2001, a few months before 9/11, Rob Hand wrote an article in *The Mountain Astrologer*. On the front page of this issue there is an image of tanks rolling through America, and when you turn to the page of the article you will see an image of the Twin Towers. In his prophetic article he suggests that the USA may be taking on the Taliban during the Saturn–Pluto opposition.

It is important to note here as well that, during the opposition and before 9/11, two airlines (Trans World Airlines, part of American Airlines, and Ansett Australia, part of Air New Zealand) had already gone bankrupt. When many flights around the globe were cancelled for some days following the attacks, this had a further effect on an already challenged aviation industry.

In recent years we have experienced the following squares between Saturn and Pluto:

15 Nov 2009	1° Libra (Saturn) and Capricorn (Pluto)
31 Jan 2010	4° Libra (Saturn) and Capricorn (Pluto)
21 Aug 2010	2° Libra (Saturn) and Capricorn (Pluto)

Since Saturn–Pluto made these squares (in tandem with other challenging planetary cycles) we have seen power struggles involving violent rioting and protests around the world. Saturn–Pluto bring fear, dread and depression, all of which are being experienced by many of us in the global population as we watch the economy as we know it plummet. We cannot be certain exactly what will come from these squares between Saturn–Pluto, and in particular their aspects to the other outer planets during the current period, because their effect will take a long time to digest and play out.

The Ingress of Neptune into Pisces

Both the zodiac sign of Pisces and its modern ruling planet Neptune are often associated with the yearning to escape from reality, dependency and addictions. When this is viewed from a mundane perspective we see dependencies and escapism within populations. A major transit to Pisces can introduce new forms of escapism, be it through entertainment such as television and games like Xbox, or in alcohol and drug use. We also see greater social neuroses and paranoia in response to world events, which are fuelled by the media.

The underdog gets more attention than usual, and issues of poverty and social alienation, as well as depression, oppression and exploitation, which have been previously hidden from society, are brought into collective awareness. The welfare system (and the taxation that pays for it) will become a concern and, along with Uranus in Aries, we may start to see some backlash for the rising unemployment. Institutions such as prisons and hospitals also come under the radar when Pisces is triggered by transiting planets.

Pisces is also associated with healing, and since Neptune's ingress into this sign in 2011 we can expect developments in orthodox medicine, through technologies and pharmaceuticals, as well as advancements in alternative health and healing. Compassion – socially and institutionally – becomes a social concern, and an example of this is just before Neptune entered Pisces (in February 2012), the UK's *The Daily Telegraph* published a headline story 'Nurses lose their compassion'.[108] What was highlighted here was the need for better care and a nicer bedside manner from those who treat the sick and vulnerable. Issues such as these will become a focus over the next fourteen years as Neptune travels through Pisces.

---

108. *The Daily Telegraph*, 'Nurses lose their compassion', 16 January 2012, p. 1.

The film industry is also governed by Pisces, and the release of the film *Inception* in 2010 is an introduction to what we can expect from Neptune arriving in Pisces, not just from a visual perspective but also conceptually. Dreams and access to the unconscious will become a focus. Pisces also represents the sea and we can expect the oceans to be a focus on the political and economic front (for example, access to water) and we can expect to learn more about the depths of the oceans – a world we know very little about.

With Neptune travelling through the final degrees of Aquarius (as well as making a conjunction to Jupiter in 2009), we witnessed radical changes in technology. Neptune has also completed several years of being in mutual reception with Uranus (as modern ruler of Aquarius) and we have had a major global focus on environmental issues, seen the growth of social networks, and an increasing world-wide dependency on television and electronic games for many, particularly children, and this is likely to increase as Neptune travels through Pisces.

The era of Neptune in Pisces will open up even more new visual instruments and modes, building on the ideas and concepts of recent times. There are no boundaries to Neptune in Pisces; it dissolves all of them, allowing for all possibilities. Along with Pluto in Capricorn and the sextile these planets will make to each other, questions about how and why we are here will be paramount – our place in the larger scheme of things will be an area of preoccupation and may lead to some interesting developments. There may be developments in answering these questions with mathematics, biology, psychology and quantum physics or astrophysics, or perhaps in a more spiritual, esoteric or religious context.

How our reality can change was a leading theme when Neptune last travelled through Pisces (1847–1862). Charles Darwin, who had Mercury, Jupiter and Pluto in Pisces, Saturn conjunct Neptune, and an Aquarian Sun, released *On The Origin of Species* in 1859, which radically changed our understanding of how we came to be and, subsequently, our world view. So we can expect questions around the 'reality' of what happens after we die, bringing in concepts of fate and belief. New possibilities or old concepts concerning the hereafter may be reconsidered and adopted. Different explanations about ultimate questions – what we are about and what we are made of – will come under the spotlight.

This period will ask us to look at our own version of reality, and perhaps with the ingress of Pluto into Capricorn and again, the Hadron Collider which is trying to find the answer to our reality we may be standing on the edge of a new version of it. A potentially interesting time will be when Neptune reaches 7° Pisces. This will make a square to the Neptune–Pluto conjunction of 1892 at 7° degrees of Gemini.

The first ingress of Neptune into Pisces occurred on 4 April 2011 (see chart overleaf). Neptune made its ingress while conjuncting to Chiron and making a wide conjunction to Venus. These three planets in the chart represent the only flexibility, as they are the only planets in mutable signs. The other seven planets are in cardinal signs, and six of these reside in Aries. This is an ambitious and driven chart; highly motivated, it gives a taste of the pioneering innovations that Neptune in Pisces will bring. There will be challenges and a suggestion of social troubles, indicated by the conjunction with Chiron.

Set for London at the moment of ingress, Neptune is placed in the seventh house – the house of partnerships – and with its conjunction to Venus may be seen to represent the Royal Wedding between Prince William and Kate Middleton later in the same month. With all those planets in Aries, it was no surprise when protesters threatened fire flares throughout the ceremony. The wedding seemed to reinstate the myth we have of relationships, a fairy story come true, and perhaps was an attempt to restore faith in the institution of marriage.

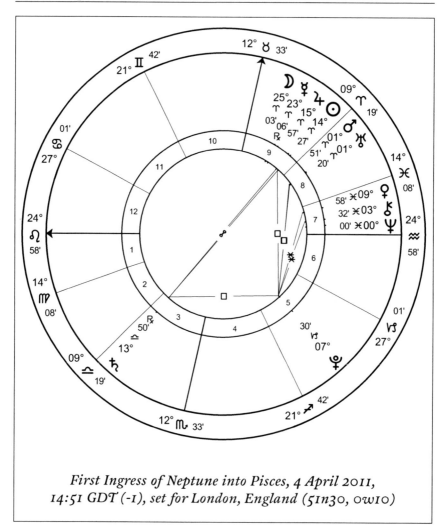

First Ingress of Neptune into Pisces, 4 April 2011,
14:51 GDT (-1), set for London, England (51n30, 0w10)

The second and final ingress of Neptune into Pisces will take place on 3 February 2012 (at the time of writing this has not yet occurred). In this chart (opposite), which is set for London, Neptune again makes its ingress into Pisces with Chiron, but this time Neptune is sextile to Jupiter, trine to Saturn (out of sign) and widely trine the Moon (out of sign). This is an easier ingress which helps to balance the opposition between Jupiter and Saturn. Neptune conjunct Chiron in the sixth house of the UK capital's ingress chart may also represent some job losses, perhaps resulting in rising unemployment.

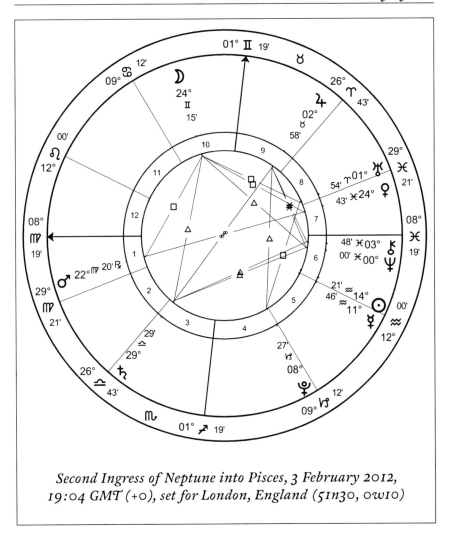

*Second Ingress of Neptune into Pisces, 3 February 2012,
19:04 GMT (+0), set for London, England (51n30, 0w10)*

Again, with the myth of Chiron we might expect that
problems and suffering of one kind or another will be in the
spotlight. The ingress sits in the sixth house and with the
harmonious aspects it makes, along with the Uranus–Pluto
square (previously conjunct in Virgo) we may see some
developments in the health and welfare system that serve
the wider public. With Neptune making an out of sign trine
to Saturn in Libra along with the Moon in Gemini, this may
have something to do with women or female health in some
way. There may also be developments with sleep and memory
recall. Interestingly, George Pullman, a Pisces, invented the

Pullman Railroad sleeping car on trains in 1856, when Jupiter was conjunct Neptune in Pisces. He wanted people to travel longer distances so invented a mechanism for them to sleep on trains!

There will be no limit to what we put our minds to understanding during the next fourteen years. The transit may suggest a greater exploration of the mind, either psychologically, spiritually or chemically. New forms of mind-altering street drugs may be created, and there will be the expansion of the pharmaceutical industry. Those who profit from the pharmaceutical industry may have it in their best interest to spread propaganda which increases paranoia about health and leads to greater drug dependency. The film *Limitless*, which was released just as Neptune made its ingress into Pisces, is an example of this. The film is about a man who becomes dependent on drugs that expand his mind and give him the ability to achieve anything, albeit at a high cost to his health. Such films (and their titles) give us some idea of the themes we can expect at this time.

Science fiction will no doubt increase in popularity on television and in film (and games), as it has the potential to expand our mind, imagination and consciousness. One of the early writers of science-fiction, Sir Jagadish Chandra Bose, was born on 30 November 1858, when Neptune was in Pisces. Neptune in his chart is at the apex of a T-square. Among his Piscean activities was his invention of the first wireless detection device; his research extended into plant life and many other innovations, and he was also the first Bengali science-fiction writer.

The sci-fi writers of yesterday have had an enormous influence on our concepts of reality (and what is not reality) and the future we create for ourselves. When we look at the science-fiction programmes of the 1960s, particularly the original *Star Trek*, it is surprising to what extent these programmes and ideas led to future inventions and our ideas about future possibilities.

Neptune in Pisces may also lead to more positive developments in alternative medicine and the care industry. In the 1850s, when Neptune last visited Pisces, there were advancements in homeopathy and the founding of the nursing industry. Louis Pasteur was born in 1822, with Sun conjunct Neptune in Capricorn. He was a chemist and microbiologist and is renowned for several Piscean pursuits such as the pasteurization of milk and wine to kill germs, improvements in the process of brewing beer, a range of vaccinations and cures, but mostly for his discovery of germ theory which, through his discovery of viruses, made enormous changes to hospitals and medical practices.

When a planet transits its own sign, the nature of the planet and sign are accentuated. Pisces and Neptune can represent what is painful and hidden from normal view, and aspects of what is hidden in society will be exposed, possibly more so when Saturn makes its ingress into Scorpio in 2012. The 1850s saw many battles for the abolition of slavery in the USA. Abraham Lincoln, born on the same day as Charles Darwin (both had Mercury, Jupiter and Pluto in Pisces, and Saturn conjunct Neptune), was elected in 1860 on an anti-slavery campaign, and brought institutionalized slavery to an end in the US. When Neptune moves through Pisces, the underdog is highlighted, and concern for those suffering or disadvantaged will be of greater concern worldwide.

Another born in this era was Rudolf Steiner, who had Sun, Mercury and Neptune in Pisces. Steiner is known for founding Anthroposophy, a spiritual and moral philosophy that extends to biodynamic agriculture, anthroposophical medicine and Waldorf education (which has over 1000 schools worldwide). With a science and theology background, Steiner succeeded in creating a synthesis between the scientific and the mystical worlds, and continues to have millions of followers worldwide today. We may expect similar themes – or perhaps even a resurgence of his philosophies – during Neptune's journey through Pisces over the next fourteen years.

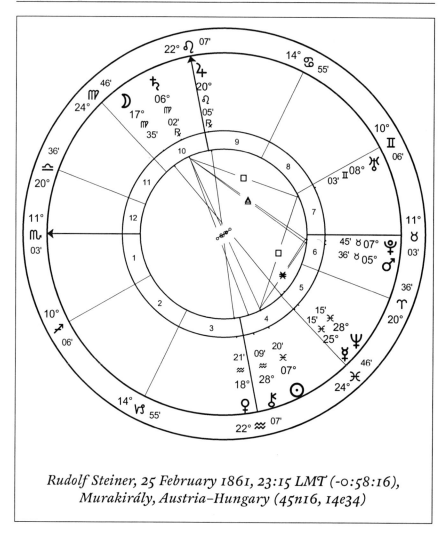

Rudolf Steiner, 25 February 1861, 23:15 LMT (-0:58:16),
Murakirály, Austria–Hungary (45n16, 14e34)

Anthroposophy is concerned with the natural sciences,
spiritual development and ethical practices. What is unique
about Steiner's philosophy is that it challenges the orthodox
perception of rational and limited imagination. With Neptune
in Pisces, new levels of perception come forth. For example,
when we assess the value of organic products we measure
the value of where and how they were grown. However, with
organics and biodynamic growing, there are life forces that
cannot be quantified or measured as it is more to do with
higher levels of perception – something you cannot (yet)

put a value on.[109] While Neptune travels through Pisces, doors will open to the individual and the collective that lead to many deeper and more imaginative ways to perceive things.

When our imagination deepens we understand ourselves in a different way. Neptune is not usually concerned with logic but more what makes universal sense and how everything is connected. Beyond the rational, it makes us think about the magic things in life, often the things that the (dogmatic) scientific view doesn't address. Examples of this will be addressing the concept of *love, déjà vu* or *afterlife experiences* (which science has not been successful in answering). A good example of this is Rupert Sheldrake's book, *Dogs That Know When Their Owners Are Coming Home*. In this book he gives several wonderful examples of animal telepathy such as a midwife (who works in various locations and inconsistent hours) whose husband always has a cup of tea ready for her as soon as she walks in the door – whatever time that may be. Her husband knows when to put the kettle on as the dog sits at the window twenty minutes before his wife returns from work. Logical explanations such as hearing the car or smell of the owner or consistent timing cannot provide an explanation here, but telepathy (or psychic knowing) seems to provide a better explanation. These are the types of areas that are developed as Neptune travels through its own sign of Pisces.

Neptune in Pisces broadens the mind and opens up the possibilities, but it also represents escape – hence why it rules drugs and alcohol – and one must be sure of how to return to practical daily life once one has fallen down the rabbit hole.

Another interesting person born during the last time Neptune was in Pisces is Emile Durkheim, commonly known as the father of sociology and the social sciences in general. Sociology is the study of post-industrial society and human interaction.

109. Conversation with biodynamic farmer, Peter White.

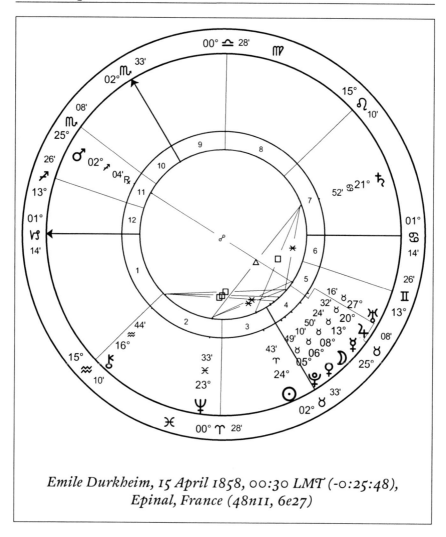

Emile Durkheim, 15 April 1858, 00:30 LMT (-0:25:48),
Epinal, France (48n11, 6e27)

In 1897, Durkheim produced the most comprehensive study ever conducted on suicide. Pisces has often been associated with suicide, which can be seen as the ultimate form of escape. Durkheim has Neptune in Pisces trine to Saturn, along with six planets in Taurus, in his natal chart. His work explores the demographic of people (including their occupation, religious affiliation, marital status and educational achievement) who are more likely to commit suicide.

His work was published while Neptune was at 22° Gemini, squaring his own natal Neptune, and while Saturn and

Uranus were conjunct at 25° Scorpio, the latter perhaps contributing to his interest in death. This groundbreaking research demonstrates a split between the psychological and sociological, demonstrating how social factors can play a large part in the analysis of suicide. While Neptune travels through Pisces (and sextiles Pluto in Capricorn), discussions about suicide, from both a psychological and sociological perspective, will probably be revisited yet again.

Water, in every respect, will no doubt be of great importance during this period. Areas under the spotlight could include the physiology of humans (who are of course made up predominantly of water); political problems leading to the shortage of water in the world; the race to desalinate sea water; increasing investment in the already multi-billion dollar bottled water industry; the pollutants and threat to endangered species in our oceans; concerns over melting polar ice caps; the threat of future tsunamis; the healing properties of water; the ownership of the seas; the tens of thousands undiscovered of species that live in the oceans, which occupy over 97 per cent of our planet's surface (in volume); and the discovery of water on other planets. Peter Batson, marine biologist and award-winning winner has stated that due to the volume of water occupying the Earth's surface, if the Earth were to be visited by beings from a different planet, they would have a higher likelihood of communicating with species in our oceans – and possibly species we do not even know exist![110]

Neptune in Pisces is inclusive and marks a period of inclusion and totality, and (coupled with Uranus square Pluto) interest in the unknown and what else is 'out there' will become a focus.

Pisces is about water but also about gases and other substances, such as nuclear power, and already this has become an area of focus. As Neptune was just about to enter Pisces in 2011,

---

110. Conversation with Peter Batson's sister, Cat Keane.

following a series of natural disasters in the region in March, the Fukushima Daiichi nuclear power plant in Japan had to be shut down, along with other power stations, due to highly dangerous radioactive leaks.[111] This was the biggest nuclear disaster since Chernobyl in 1986.

Neptune in Pisces will no doubt be a marker for injecting some magic into our routine and fast-paced life style. With the possible introduction of telepathic technologies, changes in sleep patterns and dream recognition and the ability to develop telepathy and possibly predict the future, Neptune in Pisces may bring huge changes to how we think and what we understand to be possible. The merging of quantitative and qualitative research will enhance how we know what we know and what we could know, allowing for a new way to interpret information and knowledge.

Logic will get you from A to B.
Imagination will take you everywhere.

Albert Einstein

---

111. *The New Zealand Herald*, 02 April 2011, p 1.

Uranus and Neptune in Mutual Reception

Uranus entered the Neptune-ruled sign of Pisces in March 2003 and travelled through this sign until March 2011 when it entered Aries. Neptune entered the Uranus-ruled sign of Aquarius in January 1998 and resided there until February 2012 when it ingressed into its own sign of Pisces. Thus, Uranus and Neptune were in mutual reception (i.e., in each other's signs) for eight years.

Several themes occurred during this mutual reception that had an impact on every culture on the planet and, arguably, had more of an influence on people's world view and the way we live than any other theme in history. This of course is also attributed to several other planetary configurations occurring (namely the cardinal T-square of 2008), but as the cardinal crisis unfolds during the Uranus–Pluto squares, what will also remain is what we gained and learnt through the recent mutual reception of Uranus and Neptune.

One of the things we learnt during this period was a wakening up to climate change and global warming. Uranus and Neptune and their respective signs are both concerned with nature and the environment, but in quite different ways. Uranus and Aquarius are concerned with the future and evolution, along with the political, social and moral responsibility we have for the planet we reside on, and the way in which we behave. Neptune and Pisces are concerned with nature from a more holistic and spiritual perspective. They are sincerely and deeply concerned with the fundamental problems that the planet is facing and are linked to our commitment to solve them. Both planets and signs represent personal and mass consciousness and have an urgent need to address planetary problems and the causes and consequences of them.

Concerns about rising sea temperatures came to our attention during this period, in particular the rapid warming in the

Arctic, where unprecedented ice melting continues to occur as the sea is warming at a faster rate than any other place on earth. This warming is directly affecting temperatures in Siberia, Alaska, Canada, Greenland and Scandinavia. Fred Pearce reports that it is predicted that by 2030 there may not be any summer ice in the Arctic at all. He tells us that this potential runaway warming will have a dire effect on the entire planet, socially and economically, and the consequences will be nothing less than catastrophic. We can expect rapid erosion, buckled highways and pipelines, collapsing buildings and drunken forests, an unmanageable amount of carbon released into the atmosphere. Changing weather patterns will render the monsoon seasons in South Asia nonexistent, which will affect water supplies and food growth for over two billion people.[112]

These issues will continually come to our attention during the Uranus–Pluto squares, along with the extinction (and discovery) of species, particularly within our oceans while Neptune resides in Pisces. The positive side of this is that our relationship with the planet will change, and we will no longer so easily strip the planet of natural resources. We will have more regard for the consequences of our actions. We will learn there is a different way to live and, with a little effort, everybody can do their bit. We will think about the planet in a different way, returning to greater respect for the sky, the land and oceans as our ancestors once had.

Another theme of the Uranus–Neptune mutual reception is the addiction (Neptune) to technology (Uranus). We now live in a world with a population of almost seven billion people. In the year 2000, 360 million people used the Internet. This had increased to well over two billion by 2011. The population during this period increased by 30.2 per cent, yet Internet users increased by 480.4 per cent.[113] The number of hours that people, in particular children, watch television

112. Fred Pearce, 'Meltdown', *New Scientist*, 28 March 2009, pp. 32–36.
113. http://www.internetworldstats.com/stats.htm [accessed 16 Nov 2011].

is of great concern, as is the amount of time children play on technological games. Adults become dependent on their phones and the applications that come with them and physical exercise is largely replaced with technological recreation and is one of the major contributors to obesity. Internet dating sites are becoming the quickest and easiest way to meet the right partner. Virtual worlds where people can either duplicate themselves or create the 'perfect you' for all age groups (particularly children) are flooded over the Internet and relationships within these virtual worlds often have more time spent on them than 'real' ones. We can expect this to expand and develop as Neptune enters Pisces and where reality and the virtual world become blurred. On a social level people have become more detached. The children of the next generation tend to prefer communicating through Facebook, BBM and MSN rather than riding their bikes around their communities. This is not necessarily a bad thing but it is changing how people interact.

People become less personal and tend to interact in groups rather than one-to-one – a characteristic of Aquarius. A major problem however is that many of these children of the next generation often measure their social popularity, for example, by how many friends they have on Facebook. They link to hundreds if not thousands of people on the Internet, and here the Uranus–Neptune mutual reception can be seen as the dissolving (Neptune) of what was once understood as a 'friend' (Aquarius) to a more universal model, which on the upside creates a vast social network but on the downside mostly extends to people who they do not really know or have never actually met.

In fact, as a society we seldom look upwards to the sky any more; we mostly look downwards, our faces reflected in our mobile phones, iPods and other gadgets. This has become a way of life for our children. The technologies we have given them are making them the programmers of the future. We might want to be careful about where this could lead, particularly with the Xbox and other electronic games, which are so readily available to our next generation. With Uranus in Aries, war becomes a focus and we can expect war programs to increase and we may need to be sure that we are not training our children to be the soldiers of tomorrow.

Jupiter, the co-ruler of Pisces, was also with Neptune during its journey through Aquarius from January 2009 to January 2010, as the economy started its domino collapse around the globe.

Ray Merriman notes that the mutual receptivity is rare for these three planets (Jupiter, Uranus and Neptune), and points out that this mutual reception has not occurred in 3,000 years except in 1843, a point in time which followed another great depression and the collapse of the US banking system.[114]

Uranus and Neptune do not bring about action, unlike astrological configurations such as the cardinal T-square. They are more of a theme that is reflected throughout a period and where slow changes in social consciousness occur. Coupled with the Uranus–Pluto squares, they are markers in history which show a period where life as we know it no longer exists after they move on.

---

114. Ray Merriman, 'Is It Camelot or an Economic Armageddon?', *The Mountain Astrologer*, June/July 2009, pp 25-32.

Chiron and Mundane Astrology

When researching the Uranus–Pluto conjunction I was so surprised by how little had been written by the 1960s on the astrology of Pluto. Of course, Pluto had only been recently discovered (in 1930) and understandably little was known or had been researched by astrologers at this point.

Similarly, since Chiron's discovery at 9:56 am on 1 November 1977, in Pasadena, California, although much has been written about the psychological or natal characteristics of the small planet, there has been less research conducted in mundane astrology. In Baigent, Campion and Harvey's *Mundane Astrology*, Chiron is described as 'still too new to have accumulated any definitive literature on its possible mundane significance',[115] and refers the reader to Zane Stein, who has since built an excellent website with years of research and informative articles about the astrological Chiron.[116]

As astrologers, we understand Chiron to be an immortal, half horse, half man, who is conceived through rape and was not acknowledged by his father (Kronus), was rejected by his mother (Philyra), and raised by Apollo who taught Chiron everything he knew. Later in life, Chiron became a powerful teacher and mentor to several of the Greek gods and was considered the wisest of all centaurs. After being accidently wounded by a poisoned arrow from Hercules (one of his students), which brought him lifelong pain, Chiron eventually traded his immortality with Prometheus. Released from his pain, Chiron was given an eternal place in the heavens and is remembered as the wounded healer.

We can understand from this that, within mundane astrology, Chiron will play a significant role in describing the ills in

115. Baigent et al., *Mundane Astrology*, p. 340.
116. http://www.zanestein.com/chiron_a.htm [accessed 04 October 2011].

society, and its astrological positioning will illustrate when and how certain pains are felt. But amongst that pain, Chiron offers a higher road, a point in time when a population can rise above, everyone can be the best that one can and where lessons are learnt.

Dennis Elwell writes eloquently on Chiron in *Cosmic Loom*, saying, 'Chiron is inculcating in humanity the belief that nothing is impossible. His specific gift is the audacity to attempt what might at first seem beyond our scope. The nerve to dare – without which all our talents and opportunities would be wasted... when you set out to do battle with giants, vanquish dragons, it doesn't pay to be overawed by the opposition. You have to refuse to be intimidated. Chiron rubs his hands with especially pleasurable anticipation when people say this or that simply can't be done.'[117] He goes on to say, 'Chiron is powerfully behind the mission of ultimately creating the superhuman out of the averagely human. Man is an unfinished being, an embryo, a transitional form.'[118]

Larry Williamson echoes Elwell in talking about Chiron's courage and telling a story of how the discovery of Chiron is about the awakening of the warrior consciousness in society.[119] Williamson talks about Chiron's discovery awakening alternative medicine and the revival of martial arts in his excellent article.

With an irregular orbit, Chiron's cycle is on average just over fifty years and as it makes its journey it orbits between Saturn and Uranus. What makes Chiron's orbit interesting with regards to the Uranus–Pluto square is that the period between the conjunctions of Uranus and Pluto in 1965 and 1966, and the squares of Uranus and Pluto from 2012 to 2015, spans almost fifty years – one full Chiron cycle. Thus,

117. Dennis Elwell, *The Cosmic Loom*, p. 96.
118. Elwell, p. 97.
119. Larry Williamson, 'Chiron: The Sacred Warrior Archetype', at: http://www.zanestein.com/chiron_a.htm [accessed 24 March 2012].

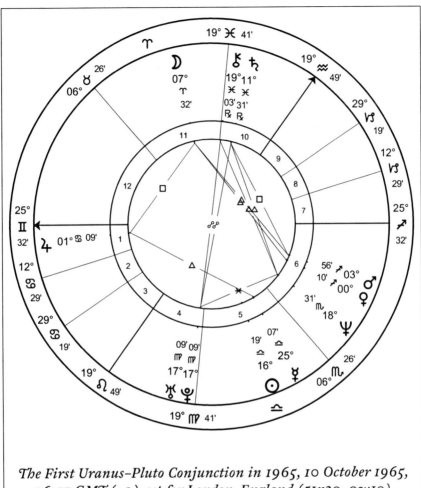

The First Uranus–Pluto Conjunction in 1965, 10 October 1965, 06:17 GMT (+0), set for London, England (51n30, 0w10). Showing the planets from Mars to Pluto

the position of Chiron in 1965 at the first conjunction at 19° Pisces will come back to this point in 2016, just after the last Uranus–Pluto square occurs.

As the Uranus–Pluto conjunction first took place in October 1965 (chart above), Chiron was widely conjunct Saturn and opposing the Uranus–Pluto conjunction, perhaps representing the social ills, challenges and rebellion that flared up at the time. Interestingly, fifty years before then – in March and April of 1915, when Chiron was at 19° Pisces – what was considered to be an epic film, *The Birth of a Nation*, a story about the rescuing qualities of the Ku Klux Klan, was banned due to its racist depictions throughout. Also at this time, heavy duty laws and pressure continued for alcohol prohibition, and the Germans had devised a new war weapon which caused further difficulties for the British and allied war effort – gas! Also evident of Chiron in Pisces, this was also when blues singing legend Billie Holiday was born (7 April 1915).

On 20 April 2009, while teaching at the Astrological Lodge of London, a discussion was recorded on the line-up of Jupiter, Chiron and Neptune in Aquarius building to a square to Mercury in Taurus. As we know in astrology, Jupiter will tend to exaggerate, Chiron wounds and teaches us lessons about suffering, and Neptune will highlight social ills. It was discussed that this challenging square between these fixed signs also had a 'flavour' of the 'foot-and-mouth' and 'mad-cow' disease that came out of the May 2000 square between Uranus in Aquarius square to the planetary line-up in Taurus (the bull) at around the same early 20s degrees. It was predicted that an infectious virus, perhaps a flu, could develop (perhaps animal-related again) and, if so, this might be announced in the UK's *Sunday Times* on 26 April 2009 as the square became exact. On 26 April 2009, it was reported in the UK *Sunday Times* and other publications around the world that there was a global outbreak of a flu pandemic, commonly known as swine flu.

The purpose of mentioning this is to illustrate that it is possible to predict events by planetary signatures but also in conjunction with other techniques such as sign degrees, which can trigger a similar event to one that has occurred before.

Chiron has spent several years travelling with Neptune and, although forming only one exact conjunction (17 February 2010) at 26° Aquarius, Chiron stays within 10 degrees of orb of Neptune from February 2007 to February 2016. When these planets come together they mark a historical period in time. They depict a time where people have suffered through war and where there has been loss on both a human and environmental level. The month of the exact conjunction saw the devastation of Haiti through the earthquake, the operation Aurora when the US fought with China over cyber attacks on Google, floods were abounding throughout this period and in the few months following, Australia, Pakistan, South America, China, Malaysia, Nigeria, South Africa, the Philippines, Western and Eastern Europe and the UK had extreme cold weather – in the UK this was called 'the big freeze'. Neptune represents water and Chiron is about suffering and the ability to survive such ills. Interestingly, during the year of the conjunction, the Oscar for Best Picture, along with eight other Oscars (and numerous other awards), was awarded to *The Hurt Locker*, a movie that conveyed the untold suffering of soldiers in Iraq. On 15 December 2011, when the war with Iraq was declared over, Neptune and Chiron were only 2 degrees apart.

Chiron's previous conjunction with Neptune was on 4 September 1945 at 5° Libra, two days after Japan officially surrendered from World War II and one month after the bombing of Hiroshima. Chiron and Neptune represent monumental moments in history, periods of sadness and suffering, and the resulting lessons to be learnt.

The Personal is Political

Firstly, before talking about any cycle it is important to understand its relevance to human society and consciousness.

'The personal is political' is a phrase that was first coined by feminists and taken up by activists in the late 1960s, and it has a historical and significant meaning for astrologers. We are all born at a point in time at which a multitude of other things is happening. This point in time not only captures the astronomy of birth but a snapshot of the cycles of cultural, political and economic thought. Generations are born into this era, carrying with it the social climate of the time. We think of history in 'times', 'periods' and 'generations' and each of us is born at a time which not only confines us but provides opportunities for the political framework in which we were born. We are all part of these continuous cycles which contribute to the present manifestations of politics and social phenomena.

Interestingly, the phrase 'the personal is political' was turned on its head in later years and many now believe that it is not the personal that is political but rather that the political is personal! Like many other astrologers, I have an interest in psychology and social and economic issues. I have always found astrology to be an interesting synthesis between the two — the great mediator between nature and nurture. Astrologers have created a consistent theoretical framework in order to understand the individual on a political level and to also understand subsequent generations based on the astronomy that they carry with them.

To understand the complexities within your natal chart it is often interesting to consider what was going on around the world when you were born. How were the astrological signatures in your birth chart acted out socially at the time you were born? What have you taken from that moment and how much of this point in history is still lived out in your own life, consciously or subconsciously?

It is interesting to read the newspapers that were printed around the time of your birth, or to search online for information about world events of the time, to see how these describe not just the mundane astrology but also the individual born into the same moment. Although you may not have contributed to the social issues that were going on, your parents were socially involved and you are a product of those times and politics too, and continue to be so.

In late April 1889, when Neptune was conjoined by Pluto, Oklahoma City and neighbouring Guthrie were formed by over 10,000 people in a rush to claim the land. Soon after, the powerful Eiffel Tower opened in Paris, thousands died when a dam flooded in Pennsylvania, and hundreds of Germans and Americans died when their ships sank in a typhoon off Samoa; in Austria, Adolf Hitler was born.

A close friend of mine who was born in March 1966 has Venus in Aquarius opposing his Leo Moon, with Jupiter in Gemini in the third house as the focal point of a T-square. Mercury, which disposits his Jupiter, is conjunct his Aries Ascendant. It is no surprise that the papers during the week of his birth were filled with headlines about the first space docking by US astronauts and about British United Airways buying and building fleets of planes to cater for cheaper holidays and speedier travel. A week later, British Airport Authorities was formed. These were quite pivotal times for how and where people could travel. From the time he was a small boy, my friend's dream was to become a pilot. It was the idea of travelling anywhere and at any time that appealed to him. He took his personal pilot's licence in his thirties, as a hobby, and it is no surprise that later in life he worked for British Airport Authorities, supporting and implementing their flight network infrastructure!

While teaching at the London School of Astrology on this subject one evening, students' birth dates were looked at in conjunction with mundane events that were occurring. One woman was born on the day the Thames river was being cleaned out and the sewers of London were being repaired. The woman was a plumber! This was not surprising either for the mundane event or the individual living out her chart with a significant number of planets in Scorpio.

One other woman was born on the day that Mahatma Gandhi died. Within the class we discussed how his death would have been felt by people in India and around the world and words such as 'despair' and 'loss of hope' were raised. What this particular student shared with the class had significant meaning regarding how the political becomes personal. She talked about her work as a psychotherapist and told us that in her work, and because of the clients she worked with, her most common offering was 'to take their hope, carry it and protect it for them until they want it returned'. When we looked at the ephemeris it was not surprising to see that on that particular day Jupiter in Sagittarius was making an opposition to Uranus in the sky.

The point of these examples is to highlight how we all carry the mundane events of our birth time with us in our own lives, irrespective of class, race or gender, and this may be borne out in a number of different ways.

Similarly, during the Uranus–Pluto squares, it is not surprising for astrologers to see clients who are having points at the early cardinal degrees of their charts being highlighted as areas of concern, in particular the luminaries and/or angles, as the Uranus–Pluto square triggers these areas of their chart. Their circumstances are always different but the themes of personal crisis are more common than not. Thus, those born around the solstices and equinoxes will be born with the Sun and possibly other planets at early cardinal degrees and will also pick up the squares that are about to occur.

Another important point to note here is that due to the unusual orbit and speed of Pluto's cycle (travelling faster through some parts of the zodiac than others), we have an older generation that is experiencing Pluto half-returns. Many of those born with Pluto in Cancer (1912–39) will have Pluto in Capricorn opposing their own natal Pluto. On a mundane level we can see the issue of an ageing society already been addressed (Capricorn is about time), and this will be felt on an individual level as well. Issues of food, family, the home and respect for one's elders will also be addressed as Pluto opposes those with Pluto in Cancer over the 2010s.

Hence, it is not just the astrological significators of the time that tell us about what is happening and about those experiencing it at the time, but also those born within that era paint us a larger picture of how that planetary cycle unfolds, how it works and is lived out on a human level.

Conclusion

These are interesting times that we are living through. The mundane planetary line-up from 2008–15 will be remembered as an era of unprecedented change. The themes will not be new, these stories have already been told; they are already familiar to us. However, how we resolve or address these themes will require new and innovative approaches.

Against the backdrop of the technological revolution that we are currently living through, while this is an exciting time in the evolution of humankind, we need to remember the observations of Dennis Elwell, who reminds us we can lose our way focusing on the method rather than the destination.[120] Moral and ethical boundaries will continue to shift throughout the Uranus–Pluto squares, as will the evaluation of risk. We are about to enter an age in which technology will permeate every aspect of our society to the extent that we are so dependent and dominated by it that we risk losing our human-ness. We might want to take a step back and see what treasures we can salvage from our past and present.

With the looming Uranus–Pluto squares, we can expect the themes which underpinned the events of the 60s to rise again, but these will be different because of the outer planet positions: Pluto in Capricorn, Uranus in Aries and Neptune in Pisces. Uranus is about humanity and equality and addresses the need for revolt and radical change. Pluto wants to purge all that is rotten and poisonous. So when these two planets came to conjunction this is what they did: they empowered and liberated our society in the 1960s. But that was a different generation. Pluto in Leo is more courageous and expressive

---

120. Dennis Elwell, *The Astrological Journal*, Winter 1965-66, p. 13.

than the Pluto in Virgo generation, which is more subtle and will deal with crisis in a more humble way. Uranus and Pluto will always be about upheaval, revolution and bring about some major transformations in several aspects of our society, but to understand how the Pluto in Virgo generation will deal with this, we first must understand the foundations on which our current society sits.

The Uranus–Pluto conjunction in the 1960s and the economic depression in the 1930s give us some idea of what to expect, and they remind us of what not to repeat. 'We need not copy what happened in the 1960s. We cannot also be liberated or freed from doing what has already been done. What we need to do is to find our own way and a way that is genuine to one's own generation.'[121]

Although Uranus and Pluto advocate a free and fair society, they are ruthless markers of times of crisis, conflict and cultural despair. Uranus in Aries and Pluto in Capricorn in square will require society to challenge the status quo and think rather laterally – out of the box – if we are to implement (and make beneficial to society) new technological and economic systems and structures.

There is not enough time here to look at all aspects of society but if you dig deep enough you will find that the conjunction of Uranus and Pluto in the 60s gave birth to a generation which has subtly permeated the characteristics of Virgo into the very fabric of our society, perhaps without realizing it.

We also know that the next generations will inherit many of the problems and the opportunities created by their parents. These are burdensome and exciting prospects. Undoubtedly, those born of the Saturn–Uranus–Neptune in Capricorn generation (born in the late 1980s and early 1990s) will be vigilant in cleaning up the mess the previous generation has made. They are also of the generation able to turn fantasy

121. A, J & R Baumgardner, *Manifesta: Young Women, Feminism and the Future.*

into reality, particularly during the sextile between Neptune in Pisces and Pluto in Capricorn. They will, however, slow things down for a period, put more emphasis on getting it right, and hopefully understand the levels of risk that changes in society bring. Pluto throughout the 2010s will trigger those born with the outer planets in Capricorn and mark a time when we need to take stock and consolidate before taking further leaps. This group will do this before handing over the reins of society to the next generations, including those born with Uranus square Pluto.

> A generation of men is like a generation of leaves; the wind scatters some leaves upon the ground, while others the burgeoning wood brings forth – and the season of spring comes on. So of men one generation springs forth and another ceases.
>
> Homer, *The Iliad*

Appendix

Astrology Symbol Keys

Planets & Luminaries	
☉	Sun
☽	Moon
☿	Mercury
♀	Venus
♂	Mars
♃	Jupiter
♄	Saturn
⚷	Chiron
♅	Uranus
♆	Neptune
♇	Pluto

Zodiac Signs		Abbreviations
♈	Aries	Ar
♉	Taurus	Ta
♊	Gemini	Ge
♋	Cancer	Cn
♌	Leo	Le
♍	Virgo	Vi
♎	Libra	Li
♏	Scorpio	Sc
♐	Sagittarius	Sg
♑	Capricorn	Cp
♒	Aquarius	Aq
♓	Pisces	Pi

Aspects		Angle
☌	Conjunction	0°
✶	Sextile	60°
□	Square	90°
△	Trine	120°
☍	Opposition	180°

Hard Aspects and Ingresses of Jupiter, Saturn, Chiron, Uranus, Neptune and Pluto, 2007–2015

♃□♅	22 January 2007	12°Sg/Pi	1 of 3
♄☍♆	28 February 2007	20°Le/Aq	1 of 2
♃□♅	11 May 2007	17°Sg/Pi	2 of 3
♄☍♆	25 June 2007	21°Le/Aq	2 of 2
♃□♅	09 October 2007	15°Sg/Pi	3 of 3
♄ Ingress	02 September 2007	0°Vi	1 of 1
♃☌♇	11 December 2007	28°Sg	1 of 1
♃ Ingress	18 December 2007	0°Cp	1 of 1
♇ Ingress	26 January 2008	0°Cp	1 of 2
♄☍♅	04 November 2008	18°Vi/Pi	1 of 5
♇ Ingress	27 November 2008	0°Cp	2 of 2
♃ Ingress	05 January 2009	0°Aq	1 of 1
♄☍♅	05 February 2009	20°Vi/Pi	2 of 5
♃☌♆	23 May 2009	26°Aq	1 of 3
♃☌♆	27 May 2009	26°Aq	1 of 3
♃☌♆	10 July 2009	26°Aq	2 of 3
♃☌♆	22 July 2009	24°Aq	2 of 3
♄☍♅	15 September 2009	24°Vi/Pi	3 of 5
♄ Ingress	29 October 2009	0°Li	1 of 2
♄□♇	15 November 2009	1°Li/Cp	1 of 3
♃☌♆	07 December 2009	21°Aq	3 of 3
♃☌♆	21 December 2009	24°Aq	3 of 3

♃ Ingress	18 January 2010		0°Pi	1 of 1
♄□♇	31 January 2010		4°Li/Cp	2 of 3
♆☌⚷	17 February 2010		26°Aq	1 of 1
⚷ Ingress	20 April 2010		0°Pi	1 of 2
♄☍♅	27 April 2010		28°Vi/Pi	4 of 5
♃☍♄	23 May 2010		27°Pi/Vi	1 of 3
♅ Ingress	28 May 2010		0°Ar	1 of 2
♃ Ingress	06 June 2010		0°Ar	1 of 2
♃☌♅	08 June 2010		0°Ar	1 of 3
♄ Ingress	21 July 2010		0°Li	2 of 2
♃□♇	25 July 2010		3°Ar/Cp	1 of 3
♄☍♅	26 July 2010		0°Li	5 of 5
♃□♇	03 August 2010		3°Ar/Cp	2 of 3
♃☍♄	16 August 2010		2°Ar/Li	2 of 3
♄□♇	21 August 2010		2°Li/Cp	3 of 3
♃☌♅	19 September 2010		28°Pi	2 of 3
♃☌♅	04 January 2011		27°Pi	3 of 3
♃ Ingress	22 January 2011		0°Ar	2 of 2
⚷ Ingress	08 February 2011		0°Pi	2 of 2
♃□♇	25 February 2011		7°Ar/Cp	3 of 3
♅ Ingress	12 March 2011		0°Ar	2 of 2
♃☍♄	28 March 2011		14°Ar/Li	3 of 3
♆ Ingress	04 April 2011		0°Pi	1 of 2
♃ Ingress	04 June 2011		0°Ta	1 of 1
♆ Ingress	03 February 2012		0°Pi	2 of 2
♃ Ingress	11 June 2012		0°Ge	1 of 1
♅□♇	24 June 2012		8°Ar/Cp	1 of 7
♃□♆	25 June 2012		3°Ge/Pi	1 of 1

♃□♅	24 July 2012	8°Ge/Pi	1 of 3
♅□♇	19 September 2012	6°Ar/Cp	2 of 7
♄ Ingress	05 October 2012	0°Sc	1 of 1
♃□♅	15 January 2013	6°Ge/Pi	2 of 3
♃□♅	27 March 2013	11°Ge/Pi	3 of 3
♅□♇	20 May 2013	11°Ar/Cp	3 of 7
♃ Ingress	26 June 2013	0°Cn	1 of 1
♃☍♇	07 August 2013	9°Cn/Cp	1 of 3
♃□♅	21 August 2013	12°Cn/Ar	1 of 3
♅□♇	01 November 2013	9°Ar/Cp	4 of 7
♃☍♇	31 January 2014	12°Cn/Cp	2 of 3
♃□♅	26 February 2014	10°Cn/Ar	2 of 3
♃□♅	20 April 2014	13°Cn/Ar	3 of 3
♃☍♇	20 April 2014	13°Cn/Cp	3 of 3
♅□♇	21 April 2014	13°Ar/Cp	5 of 7
♃ Ingress	16 July 2014	0°Le	1 of 1
♅□♇	15 December 2014	12°Ar/Cp	6 of 7
♄ Ingress	23 December 2014	0°Sg	1 of 2
♅□♇	17 March 2015	15°Ar/Cp	7 of 7
♃□♄	03 August 2015	28°Le/Sc	1 of 1
♃ Ingress	11 August 2015	0°Vi	1 of 1
♃☍♆	17 September 2015	7°Vi/Pi	1 of 1
♄ Ingress	18 September 2015	0°Sg	2 of 2
♃☍♅	03 November 2015	17°Vi/Pi	1 of 3
♄□♆	26 November 2015	7°Sg/Pi	1 of 3

Uranus–Pluto Aspects 1850 to 2104

♅ ☌ ♇	26 June 1850	29°Ar39' D	29°Ar39' D
♅ ☌ ♇	25 September 1850	29°Ar20' R	29°Ar20' R
♅ ☌ ♇	23 March 1851	28°Ar42' D	28°Ar42' D
♅ ✶ ♇	17 September 1868	16°Cn52' D	16°Ta52' R
♅ ✶ ♇	11 January 1869	15°Cn08' R	15°Ta08' R
♅ ✶ ♇	11 July 1869	17°Cn45' D	17°Ta45' D
♅ □ ♇	21 October 1876	24°Le02' D	24°Ta02' R
♅ □ ♇	12 February 1877	22°Le37' R	22°Ta37' D
♅ □ ♇	25 August 1877	25°Le31' D	25°Ta31' D
♅ △ ♇	9 November 1884	01°Li25' D	01°Ge25' R
♅ △ ♇	29 March 1885	00°Li32' R	00°Ge32' D
♅ △ ♇	21 September 1885	03°Li03' D	03°Ge03' R
♅ ☍ ♇	31 January 1901	15°Sg49' D	15°Ge49' R
♅ ☍ ♇	29 April 1901	16°Sg17' R	16°Ge18' D
♅ ☍ ♇	17 December 1901	17°Sg33' D	17°Ge33' R
♅ ☍ ♇	28 June 1902	18°Sg35' R	18°Ge35' D
♅ ☍ ♇	06 November 1902	19°Sg18' D	19°Ge18' R
♅ △ ♇	17 March 1921	06°Pi48' D	06°Cn48' R
♅ △ ♇	25 July 1921	09°Pi00' R	09°Cn00' D
♅ △ ♇	06 February 1922	08°Pi18' D	08°Cn18' R
♅ △ ♇	18 September 1922	11°Pi06' R	11°Cn06' D
♅ △ ♇	27 December 1922	10°Pi16' D	10°Cn16' R

⛢ □ ♇	21 April 1932	20°Ar01' D	20°Cn01' D
⛢ □ ♇	02 September 1932	22°Ar54' R	22°Cn54' D
⛢ □ ♇	08 March 1933	21°Ar22' D	21°Cn22' R
⛢ □ ♇	05 November 1933	24°Ar44' R	24°Cn44' R
⛢ □ ♇	18 January 1934	23°Ar34' D	23°Cn34' R
⛢ ✶ ♇	10 June 1943	05°Ge31' D	05°Le31' D
⛢ ✶ ♇	11 October 1943	08°Ge32' R	08°Le33' D
⛢ ✶ ♇	14 April 1944	06°Ge24' D	06°Le24' R
⛢ ☌ ♇	09 October 1965	17°Vi09' D	17°Vi09' D
⛢ ☌ ♇	04 April 1966	16°Vi28' R	16°Vi27' R
⛢ ☌ ♇	30 June 1966	16°Vi06' D	16°Vi06' D
⛢ ✶ ♇	10 April 1995	00°Aq12' D	00°Sg13' R
⛢ ✶ ♇	08 August 1995	27°Cp49' R	27°Sc48' R
⛢ ✶ ♇	08 March 1996	03°Aq06' D	03°Sg06' R
⛢ ✶ ♇	20 September 1996	00°Aq47' R	00°Sg47' D
⛢ ✶ ♇	05 February 1997	05°Aq19' D	05°Sg19' D
⛢ □ ♇	24 June 2012	08°Ar23' D	08°Cp23' R
⛢ □ ♇	19 September 2012	06°Ar57' R	06°Cp57' D
⛢ □ ♇	20 May 2013	11°Ar14' D	11°Cp14' R
⛢ □ ♇	01 November 2013	09°Ar26' R	09°Cp25' D
⛢ □ ♇	21 April 2014	13°Ar34' D	13°Cp34' R
⛢ □ ♇	15 December 2014	12°Ar35' R	12°Cp35' D
⛢ □ ♇	17 March 2015	15°Ar18' D	15°Cp18' D

♅ △ ♇	18 July 2026	04°Ge29' D	04°Aq29' R
♅ △ ♇	29 November 2026	03°Ge31' R	03°Aq31' D
♅ △ ♇	15 June 2027	06°Ge51' D	06°Aq52' R
♅ △ ♇	13 January 2028	06°Ge20' R	06°Aq20' D
♅ △ ♇	10 May 2028	08°Ge49' D	08°Aq49' R
♅ ☍ ♇	22 September 2046	03°Vi45' D	03°Pi45' R
♅ ☍ ♇	15 February 2047	04°Vi42' R	04°Pi42' D
♅ ☍ ♇	16 August 2047	05°Vi54' D	05°Pi54' R
♅ ☍ ♇	11 April 2048	07°Vi27' R	07°Pi27' D
♅ ☍ ♇	30 June 2048	07°Vi59' D	07°Pi59' R
♅ △ ♇	18 December 2063	24°Sc28' D	24°Pi28' D
♅ △ ♇	28 March 2064	26°Sc22' R	26°Pi22' D
♅ △ ♇	31 October 2064	25°Sc53' D	25°Pi53' R
♅ △ ♇	31 May 2065	28°Sc44' R	28°Pi44' D
♅ △ ♇	15 September 2065	27°Sc55' D	27°Pi55' R
♅ □ ♇	15 February 2073	05°Cp17' D	05°Ar17' D
♅ □ ♇	06 April 2073	06°Cp27' D	06°Ar28' D
♅ □ ♇	13 December 2073	05°Cp44' D	05°Ar44' R
♅ □ ♇	26 June 2074	08°Cp51' R	08°Ar51' D
♅ □ ♇	24 October 2074	07°Cp23' D	07°Ar23' R
♅ ✶ ♇	20 March 2083	16°Aq25' D	16°Ar25' D
♅ ✶ ♇	28 May 2083	17°Aq56' R	17°Ar56' D
♅ ✶ ♇	09 January 2084	16°Aq22' D	16°Ar22' D
♅ ✶ ♇	07 September 2084	19°Aq00' R	18°Ar59' R
♅ ✶ ♇	28 October 2084	18°Aq03' D	18°Ar03' R
♅ ☌ ♇	24 April 2104	07°Ta35' D	07°Ta35' D

Bibliography

Anonymous, *Chronicle of the 20th Century* (London: Dorling Kindersley, 1995).

Anonymous, 'Editorial', *The Economist,* 14 April 2005, p. 2.

Anonymous, 'Spaceship Two', *The Economist,* 14 October 2010.

Arroyo, Stephen and Liz Greene, *New Insights in Modern Astrology* (Sebastopol: CRCS Publications, 1984).

Baigent, Michael, Nicholas Campion and Charles Harvey, *Mundane Astrology: An Introduction to the Astrology of Nations and Groups* (London: Thorsons, 1984).

Baumgardner, A, J and R, *Manifesta: Young Women, Feminism and the Future* (New York: Farrar, Straus and Giroux, 2000).

Campion, Nicholas, 'Revolutionary Years and the Uranus–Pluto Cycle', *The Mountain Astrologer*, Aug/Sep 2011, Issue 158, p. 32.

Chamberlain, G, E Philipp, B Howlett and K Masters, *British Births 1970* (London: William Heinemann Medical Books Ltd, 1978).

Clifford, Frank C, *British Entertainers: The Astrological Profiles* (London: Flare Publications, 2003).

Elwell, Dennis, *Cosmic Loom: The New Science of Astrology* (London, The Urania Trust, 1987).

Grint, K, *The Sociology of Work,* 3ʳᵈ Edition (Cambridge: Polity Press, 2005).

Hinisch, Carol, 'The Personal is Political' (1969), in Shulamith Firestone and Anne Koedt (Eds.), *Notes from the Second Year: Women's Liberation* (New York: Radical Feminism, 1970).

Huxley, Aldous, *Brave New World* (London: Vintage, 2007 [1932]).

Jonsson, Asgeir, *Why Iceland?* (McGraw-Hill, 2009).

Kaiser, IH and F Halberg, 'Circadian Periodic Aspects of Birth', *Annals of the New York Academy of Sciences,* 1962, Vol. 98, pp. 1056-1068.

Kambayashi, Satoshi, 'Fumbling Towards a Truce', *The Economist,* 14 October 2010.

Katz Rothman, Barbara, *Genetic Maps and Human Imaginations: The Limits of Science in Understanding Who We Are* (New York: WW Norton and Company Inc., 1998).

Kitzinger, Sheila, *The Politics of Birth* (London: Elsevier, 2005). Lewis, Michael, *Boomerang* (New York: WW Norton & Company Inc., 2011).

Lupton, Deborah, *Medicine as Culture* (London: Sage, 2006).

MacFarlane, A, E Hawe and J Bithell, 'Daily seasonal variation in live births, stillbirths and infant mortality in England and Wales, 1979–96', *Health Statistics Quarterly,* 2001, Vol. 9, pp. 5-15.

Marrs, Tim, 'A Worm in the Centrifuge', *The Economist,* 30 September 2010.

Merriman, Raymond, 'Is It Camelot or an Economic Armageddon?', *The Mountain Astrologer*, June/July 2009, pp. 25-32.

Michelson, Neil, *Tables of Planetary Phenomena* (New Hampshire: Starcraft Publishing, 2007).

Moore, Thomas, 'Caesarean births to be allowed on request', *Sky News*, UK, 23 November 2011.

Nettleton, Sarah, and Jonathan Watson, *Body in Everyday Life* (London: Psychology Press, 1998).

Pearce, Fred, 'Meltdown', *New Scientist*, 28 March 2009, pp. 32–36.

Penzias, AA & RW Wilson, 'A Measurement of Excess Antenna Temperature at 4080 Mc/s', *Astrophysical Journal*, 1965, Vol. 142, pp. 419-421.

Ray, Robin, 'Is Iceland a Ticking Time Bomb?', *Association of Professional Astrologers International (APAI) Newsletter*, Summer 2010.

Ridder-Patrick, Jane, *A Handbook of Medical Astrology* (London: Arkana, 1990).

Roberts, JM, *The New Penguin History of the World* (Penguin, 2007).

Silverstone, Matthew, *Blinded by Science* (Lloyds World Publishing, 2011).

Skinner, Christeen, *The Financial Universe: Planning your Investments using Astrological Forecasting* (Brighton: The Alpha Press, 2004).

Smith, R, 'First Womb Transplants', *Evening Standard*, London, 04 September 2006, p. 1.

Stacey, Wendy, 'Pluto in Capricorn: The Map Becomes the Territory' (Lecture at ISAR, Denver, USA, 2005).

Stacey, Wendy, 'Pluto in Capricorn' (Lecture at the Astrological Lodge of London, 2006).

Stacey, Wendy, 'Pearls of Tomorrow', *The Astrological Journal*, July/August 2010, Vol. 52, no. 4, pp. 27-34.

Stacey, Wendy, 'The Property Market Lecture' (London School of Astrology, 19 October 2008).

Steer, P, 'Caesarean section: an evolving procedure?', *British Journal of Obstetrics and Gynaecology*, 1998, Vol. 105, no. 10, pp. 1052-5.

Tarnas, Richard, *The Passion of the Western Mind; Understanding the Ideas That Have Shaped Our World View* (New York: Harmony Books, 1991).

Tarnas, Richard, *Cosmos and Psyche; Intimations of a New World View* (Viking Penguin, 2006).

Templeton, Sarah-Kate, 'All Women get right to Caesareans', *The Sunday Times*, UK, 30 October 2011, p. 1.

Tompkins, Sue, *Aspects in Astrology: A Comprehensive Guide to Interpretation* (Dorset: Element Books, 1989).

Weiss, Phoebe, 'The Neptune–Chiron Conjunction in Pisces', *The Astrological Journal*, 2011, Vol 53, Number 3.

Wells, HG, *The Shape of Things to Come* (London: Gollancz, 1933).

Williamson, Larry, 'Chiron: The Sacred Warrior Archetype', at: http://www.zanestein.com/chiron_a.htm [accessed 24 March 2012].

Young, Michael, *The Metronomic Society: Natural Rhythms and Human Timetables* (Massachusetts: Harvard University Press, 1988).

Young, S and D Concar, 'These Cells Were Made for Learning', *New Scientist Supplement*, 21 November 1992.

Websites
See the footnotes for the full title and address of the web pages consulted, and the date they were last accessed.

Birth Data

Chapter: The Uranus–Pluto Landscape of Today

First Ingress Pluto in Capricorn (set for London): 26 January 2008, 02:38 GMT (+0), London, England (51n30, 0w10).

Second Ingress Pluto in Capricorn (set for Hadron Collider location): 27 November 2008, 02:03 CET (-1), near Geneva, Franco-Swiss border (46n14, 6e03).

First Ingress Uranus in Aries (set for London): 28 May 2010, 02:44 GDT (-1), London, England (51n30, 0w10).

Second Ingress Uranus in Aries (set for London): 12 March 2011, 00:50 GMT (+0), London, England (51n30, 0w10).

Martin Luther King, Jr.: 15 January 1929, 12:00 CST (+6), Atlanta, Georgia, USA (33n45, 84w23). Source: From his mother, 'high noon', as quoted by Ruth Dewey from DELL 9/1970. Sy Scholfield quotes 'The Papers of Martin Luther King, Jr., Vol. 7', by Clayborne Carson (University of California Press, 1992), p. 1, 'about noon'. (Michael King Jr.). RR: A.

Nobel Peace Prize awarded to Martin Luther King, Jr.: 14 October 1964, Oslo, Norway (59n55, 10e45). Set for noon CET (-1).

Nelson Mandela: 18 July 1918, 14:54 EET (-2), Umtata, South Africa (31s35, 28e47). Source: Time of 'afternoon', from his entourage to Frances McEvoy's son and daughter-in-law; rectified by Noel Tyl. RR: DD.

Transits for Nelson Mandela's imprisonment: 12 June 1964, Pretoria, South Africa (25s45, 28e10). Set for noon EET (-2).

Transits for Nelson Mandela's presidential inauguration: 10 May 1994, Pretoria, South Africa (25s45, 28e10). Set for noon EET (-2).

Rodney King: 2 April 1965, 07:00 PST (+8), Sacramento, California, USA (38n34, 121w29). Source: Birth certificate quoted by Lois Rodden. (Rodney Glenn King). RR: AA.

Transits for beating of Rodney King: 3 March 1991, 00:53 PST (+8), Los Angeles, California, USA (34n03, 118w14). Source: News reports. RR: B.

LA Riots: 29 April 1992, 17:00 PDT (+7), Los Angeles, California, USA (34n03, 118w14). Source: News reports. RR: B.

Solar Eclipse (set for London): 9 March 2016, 01:54 GMT (+0), London, England (51n30, 0w10).

Chart information from Nick Campion's The Book of World Horoscopes:

Iceland Sovereignty: 1 December 1918, Reykjavik, Iceland (64n09, 21w51). Set for noon (+1).

Iceland Republic: 17 June 1944, 14:00 EGST (+0), Reykjavik, Iceland (64n09, 21w51).

UK 1066: 25 December 1066, 12:00 LMT (+0:00:40), London, England (51n30, 0w10).

UK 1801: 1 January 1801, 00:00 LMT (+0:00:36), Westminster, England (51n30, 0w09).

Libya Independence: 24 December 1951, 00:00 CEDT (-2), Tripoli, Libya (32n54, 13e11).

Libya Republic: 3 September 1969, 06:30 EET (-2), Tripoli, Libya (32n54, 13e11).

Tunisia: 15 June 1956, 17:00 CET (-1), Tunis, Tunisia (36n48, 10e11).

Egypt: 14 March 1922, 22:43 EET (-2), Cairo, Egypt (30n03, 31e15).

Syria: 1 January 1944, 00:00 EET (-2), Damascus, Syria (33n30, 36e18).

Ireland 1: 24 April 1916, 12:25 LMT (+0:25), Dublin, Ireland (53n20, 6w15).

Portugal Revolution: 4 October 1910, 11:00 LMT (+0:36:32), Lisbon, Portugal (38n43, 9w08).

Portugal Democratic Regime: 25 April 1974, 17:15 CET (-1), Lisbon, Portugal (38n43, 9w08).

Greece Revolution: 25 March 1821, 12:00 LMT (-1:28:24), Kalavryta, Greece (38n01, 22e06).

Greece Independence: 13 January 1822, 12:00 LMT (-1:34:52), Athens, Greece (37n58, 23e43).

Greece Kingdom: 3 February 1830, 12:00 LMT (-1:34:52), Athens, Greece (37n58, 23e43).

Greece Democracy: 24 July 1974, 04:00 EET (-2), Athens, Greece (37n58, 23e43).

USA Sibly: 4 July 1776, 17:10 LMT (+5) Philadelphia, Pennsylvania (39n57, 75w10).

India Republic: 26 January 1950, 10:15 INT (-5:30) Delhi, India (28n40 77e13).

People's Republic of China: 21 September 1949, Set for Noon, CCT (-8) Peking, China (39n55 116e25).

Other data

Charles Lindbergh: 4 February 1902, 01:30 CST (+6), Detroit, Michigan, USA (42n19, 83w02). Source: Family archives cited in the biography *Lindbergh* by A. Scott Berg (Berkley Trade, 1999), pp. 25-26. (Charles Augustus Lindbergh). RR: AA.

Republic of Ireland Act (signed into law): 21 December 1948, Dublin, Ireland (53n20, 6w15). Time unknown. Source: News reports. RR: B.

IMF: 27 December 1945, afternoon EST (+5), Washington, DC, USA (38n53, 77w02). Source: Sy Scholfield quotes *New York Times*, 28 December 1945, p. 1, agreements signed in the 'afternoon'. RR: B.

Euro currency commenced: 1 January 1999, 00:01 CET (-1), Frankfurt-am-Main, Germany (50n07, 8e40). Source: News reports. RR: B.

Euro currency circulated: 1 January 2002, 00:01 CET (-1), Brussels, Belgium (50n50, 4e20). Source: News reports. RR: B.

Chapter: Back to the Future

David Cameron: 9 October 1966, 06:00 GDT (-1), London, England (51n30, 0w10). Source: From him to astrologer Annabel Herriott in 2005. (David William Donald Cameron). RR: A.

Nick Clegg: 7 January 1967, 05:30 GMT (+0), Chalfont St Giles, England (51n38, 0w34). Source: From him via his secretary to Mary English by e-mail. (Nicholas William Peter Clegg). RR: A.

Lena Zavaroni: 4 November 1963, 00:45 GMT (+0),
Greenock, Scotland (55n57, 4w45). Source: Birth certificate
quoted by Caroline Gerard. (Lena Hilda Zavaroni). RR:
AA.

Richard Branson: 18 July 1950, 07:00 GDT (-1), Blackheath,
England (51n28, 0w00). Source: His PA Saskia Kitchen
to Frank Clifford, quoting Branson's mother. (Richard
Charles Nicholas Branson). RR: A.

JK Rowling: 31 July 1965, Yate, England (51n32, 2w25).
Chart set for noon with 0° Aries Ascendant. Source: Birth
certificate reproduced in *JK Rowling: A Biography* by Sean
Smith (Michael O'Mara, 2001), p. 19. (Joanne Rowling).
RR: X.

Diana, Princess of Wales: 1 July 1961, 19:45 GDT (-1),
Sandringham, England (52n50, 0e30). Source: From Diana
to her astrologer-friend Debbie Frank, and from Diana's
mother to Charles Harvey. (Diana Frances Spencer). RR: A.

Twiggy: 19 September 1949, 01:25 GDT (-1), Neasden,
London, England (51n33, 0w16). Source: In *British
Entertainers*, Frank Clifford quotes this rectification by
Penny Thornton in her book *Romancing the Stars*, p. 264;
Twiggy 'maintains it was the very early hours of the
morning'. (Lesley Hornby). RR: C.

Michael Jackson (Michael Joseph Jackson): 29 August 1958,
Gary, Indiana, USA (41n35, 87w20). Chart set for noon.
Source: Various biographies. RR: X.

Madonna: 16 August 1958, 07:05 EST (+5), Bay City,
Michigan, USA (43n35, 83w53). Source: Birth record
quoted to Tashi Grady by Madonna's father, who called
the hospital. (Madonna Louise Ciccone). RR: AA.

Chapter: Other Planetary Cycles

First Ingress Neptune in Pisces (set for London): 4 April 2011, 14:51 GDT (-1), London, England (51n30, 0w10).

Second Ingress Neptune in Pisces (set for London): 3 February 2012, 19:04 GMT (+0), London, England (51n30, 0w10).

Rudolf Steiner: 25 February 1861, 23:15 LMT (-0:58:16), Murakirály, Austria-Hungary [now Kraljevica, Croatia] (45n16, 14e34). Source: Marion March quotes birth record cited in *Rudolph Steiner* by Gerhard Wehr (Frieberg, 1983). Astrodatabank has a copy on file of a letter written to Nandan Bosma from Steiner giving his own data as 25 February 1861, 23:07 LMT. The baptism record gives a birth date of 27 February but was issued many years after Steiner's birth. (Rudolf Joseph Lorenz Steiner). RR: XX.

Emile Durkheim: 15 April 1858, 00:30 LMT (-0:25:48), Epinal, France (48n11, 6e27). Source: Sy Scholfield cites the birth certificate, as quoted in the biography *Emile Durkheim and the Reformation of Sociology* by Stjepan Gabriel Mestrovic (Rowman & Littlefield, 1993), p. 23. RR: AA.

The first Uranus–Pluto conjunction (set for London): 9 October 1965, 21:16:42 BST (-1), London, England (51n30, 0w10).

Other birth data

Sir Jagadish Chandra Bose: 30 November 1858, Bikrampur, Bengal [now Munshiganj, Bangladesh] (23n33, 90e32). Source: Various biographies. RR: X.

Charles Darwin: 12 February 1809, Shrewsbury, England (52n43, 2w45). Source: Various biographies. (Charles Robert Darwin). RR: X.

Abraham Lincoln: 12 February 1809, Sinking Spring Farm [now Hodgenville], Kentucky, USA (37n34, 85w44). Source: Various biographies. RR: X.

George Pullman: 3 March 1831, Brocton, New York, USA (42n23, 79w26). Source: Various biographies. (George Mortimer Pullman). RR: X.

Louis Pasteur: 27 December 1822, 02:00 LMT (-0:22), Dole, France (47n06, 5e30). Source: Birth certificate quoted by Michel and Françoise Gauquelin. RR: AA.

About the Author

Wendy Stacey, BA, MA, Dip. LSA, has been learning astrology since 1987, when she was 19. She considers astrology to be a lifetime apprenticeship. She has been consulting, teaching and researching professionally since 1989.

Wendy is also the author of *Consulting with Astrology: A Quick Guide to Building Your Practice and Profile*, published in September 2011.

In 2007, Wendy facilitated the rewrite of both the certificate and diploma course for The Mayo School of Astrology and wrote much of the modernized syllabus material. Her book, *Unaspected Planets*, is due for publication in 2013. Wendy writes a regular column for students in *The Astrological Journal* and has written articles for astrological publications around the globe. Her articles have been translated into several languages.

Wendy has also lectured at astrological conferences and schools in many countries, including the UK, the USA, New Zealand, Greece and Turkey.

She has spoken on several radio stations in the UK, USA and Canada. She has appeared on television talking about the Saturn return on the programme 'Quarter Life Crisis', discussing the ingress of Pluto into Capricorn on 'Spirit and Destiny' in the USA, and in April 2011 she covered the wedding of Prince William to Kate Middleton on ABC's 'Good Morning America'. Her article on the royal wedding was syndicated by the Associated Press to over 2,000 newspapers around the world.

Wendy is the current Chair of the Astrological Association of Great Britain, a position she has held since 2002 (she was the

Treasurer from 1999–2002), and has been the Principal of the Mayo School of Astrology since 2007. She is also a teacher for the London School of Astrology (from which she holds a diploma) and taught voluntarily for the Astrological Lodge of London from 2007–10.

Wendy was one of the first students and graduates to have completed the Master of Arts in Cultural Astronomy and Astrology at Bath Spa University in 2003.

At the time of publication, Wendy is in her final year at Southampton University completing a PhD in Sociology, exploring changing birth methods and, consequently, birth times.

Wendy has run a property development business since 1998, in which she redesigns the structure of properties to accommodate modern living.

Wendy currently lives in Buckinghamshire, UK, where she runs an astrological consultancy and lives with her husband and two children.

Her website can be found at *www.wendystacey.com* and her email address is wendy@wendystacey.com

About the Mayo School of Astrology

Website: www.mayoastrology.com
Email: enquires@mayoastrology.com
Telephone: (++44) 0208 997 7297

The Mayo School of Astrology offers Certificate and Diploma courses through distance learning, and is recognized as one of the foremost and internationally acclaimed astrology correspondence schools. Established in 1973 by Jeff Mayo, the school is based in London, UK, and provides online study to students around the world.

We pride ourselves on offering a broad syllabus of astrological education which gives a thorough grounding in the essentials of astrology, while ensuring that our courses are enjoyable and stimulating for students. We are continually revising and updating our syllabus to improve the courses for our students from all over the globe.

Online classes/webinars

The Mayo School also offers online classes. These are additional but complementary to the Certificate and Diploma courses. Each term offers several two-hour classes on a variety of astrological topics given by leading astrologers. Each seminar is available to Mayo students, graduates and to the general public. Further information can be found on the Mayo website at http://www.mayoastrology.com/astrology_online_classes.html130

The Mayo School offers three courses:

The Certificate Course
This is a basic course for students who have little or no knowledge of astrology. Here you will be introduced to the basic foundation of astrology, including the planets, signs and houses, aspects, interpretation, mundane and history,

as well as basic chart calculation. There are twenty-four test papers for this course.

The Certificate in Astrology Course at the Mayo School of Astrology is designed to give students a good grounding in the fundamental principles of astrology. If you enrol as a student for the Certificate Course you will be taught a broad syllabus from which astrological theories are based, along with the fundamentals of chart interpretation. We aim to educate students about the cycles which astrologers use in their art and science. You will learn how to calculate charts for births anywhere on earth, and to interpret these in terms of potential psychological traits. Students can expect to be proficient in basic astrological interpretation by the end of the third term.

The course aims to stimulate, encourage and inspire students and teach them to the highest standard. Students are expected to apply themselves to the material and test papers provided while, we hope, enjoying their studies and all aspects of the course.

The Certificate in Astrology Course is structured into three terms and is designed for you to study at your own pace. You will, however, need to complete the Certificate within twelve months of enrolment. You will be allowed to work on test papers at a level appropriate to your ability to absorb what is taught. The average time taken to complete the course is between nine and twelve months, although some students have comfortably completed it in six months.

The Advanced Certificate Course
This is the same course as the Certificate Course but designed for students with some knowledge of the planets, signs and houses. There are sixteen test papers for this course as students are not required to complete the first eight test papers of the Certificate course. The Advanced Certificate Course is designed for students who wish to fast-track to complete the Certificate or refresh their astrological knowledge and who

usually wish to enrol in the Diploma Course. Although only sixteen papers are required, all readings for the Certificate Course are provided as a refresher.

The Diploma Course
The course is for students with a basic knowledge of chart interpretation and chart calculation. This course will introduce students to more advanced areas of chart calculation and interpretation, looking at areas such as forecasting and synastry (relationships), advanced mundane and astrological techniques. There are twenty-four test papers and a final project is required for completion of this course.

The Diploma in Astrology Course is designed to give sound training in all advanced aspects of interpretation and applying the astrological craft to the highest standard. The course can take up to two years to complete, although many students comfortably complete it in less time. The compulsory papers are set over four terms. These terms have no set dates and can be started and completed within your own time frame. However, it is expected that each term's work be completed within six to ten months.

The Mayo School Diploma Course is unique and compares with no other because it offers the option to graduate in either natal (psychological) or mundane (social and world) astrology. Although students will be exposed to and expected to learn the full syllabus, the final project required for the Diploma will be in either natal or mundane astrology, at the choice of the student. There are no examinations for the Diploma Course.

A candidate who shows above-average ability will be awarded the Diploma with Credit. When an exceptionally high standard is achieved, the Diploma will be awarded with a Merit or Distinction. Candidates who wish to submit a project for both natal and mundane astrology will be awarded the Diploma with Honours.

Students who fail the course will be eligible to resit the test papers and redo the project two more times only, and within three years of enrolment.

The Diploma Course of the Mayo School of Astrology will be of considerable value to you if you intend to continue your studies in astrology, embark on professional consultancy work, research, write, teach, enter the media or use astrology alongside other professional practices such as business or health. The Mayo syllabus is also designed to equip graduates to use astrological principles to understand social, global and economic phenomena.

Each term's teachings and test papers must be studied and completed in numerical order. The syllabus is designed to expand your knowledge through the building blocks of each term's studies and to prepare you for the final project, which is set by the school each year, and is required for graduation. The prerequisites for enrolling on the Diploma are either the completion of the Mayo Certificate Course, the Mayo Advanced Preparatory Course, or an equivalent. Students who have had no formal training but who can demonstrate sound knowledge of chart calculation and interpretation will also be considered for the Mayo School of Astrology Diploma Course.

Online/Web conferences

Each year the Mayo School offers a one-day online conference for students and the public. The conference is held for those who wish to extend their knowledge in astrology, attend a variety of lectures led by renowned astrologers, and to interact and join in virtually with other astrologers around the world.

Annual conference

Each year, the Mayo School of Astrology and the London School of Astrology hold the Astrology Student Conference in London both for students of the two schools and the general public.

Our goal each year is to give students and practitioners of astrology – and anyone else who is interested in the art – a full and diverse programme of lectures and the chance to interact, network and mingle with students from various schools, the speakers and professional astrologers from our community.

Further information can be found at the Mayo website or the Astrology Student Conference website at *www.astroconference. com*

Index

Afghanistan	170, 177, 179
Africa	28
South Africa	38, 90–4, 164
North(ern) Africa	65, 67, 178, 201, 223–4
African American	90
African National Congress	91
Ageing	
society	46, 206
process	127
Agriculture	48, 51, 72, 114, 139, 141, 187
Alaska	194
Algeria	28
Andrews, Julie	144–5
Angola	38
Anthroposophy	187–8
Apartheid	91, 93
Apocalypse	15, 28, 52, 86
Arab states	29
Arctic	193–4
Aryan(ism)	20, 25, 40
Asia (n)	91
Asian Subcontinent	40
South Asia	194
Assange, Julian	60
Astrological Association, The	11, 230
Astrological Lodge of London	200, 221, 231
Austria	188, 204, 228
Balloon flight	56–7, 138
Banking	79–84, 104, 196
Berlin Wall	29, 177
Bewitched	144
Big Bang Cosmology Theory	31, 51
Big Brother	45, 103
Biodynamic farming	187–9
Birth of a Nation, The	200
Bonnie and Clyde	42
Branson, Sir Richard	31, 137–8, 227

Brave New World	41, 219
Bretton Woods Agreement	49
Caesarean sections	128–32, 220–1
California(n)	90, 95, 97, 144, 197, 223–4,
Cameron, David	71, 119, 170, 226
Campion, Nicholas	11–13, 29, 81, 175, 197, 218, 224
Canada	72, 194, 230
Capitalism	28–9, 39, 49, 100, 102, 110
Cardinal	
climax	15, 63–4, 72, 74, 77–8, 104, 152
crisis	43, 72, 101, 193
square	39
Caribbean	28
Charles, Prince of Wales	38
Childbirth	127, 129–30, 132
Chile	33, 172
China, People's Republic of	29, 32, 38, 40, 46, 50, 65, 74, 76–7, 131, 170–1, 201, 226
Christian(ity)	115, 144
Christian Science	144
Churchill, Winston	164
Civil Rights Movement	28–31, 88–90
Climate change	49, 52, 193
Clone	32, 128
Dolly the sheep	32–3, 37
Cold War, The	28, 170, 177
Communism	28–9
Cuban Missile Crisis	28
de Klerk, Frederik Willem	93
Death penalty	37–8
Debt	63–5, 77–8, 83–5, 102, 107, 171, 175
Deepwater Horizon oil spill	164
Democracy	28, 66, 68, 87, 172–3, 225
Diana, Princess of Wales	38, 149
DNA	23, 56, 128, 133
Dragons' Den	103
Drug(s)	30, 181, 186, 189
Duggan, Mark	87
Durkheim, Emile	189–90, 228
Dylan, Bob	21

Earhart, Amelia	56
Earth	
planet	13, 31, 34, 41, 191
element	109–10, 139, 162–4
sign	20, 113–14, 124, 141–2
Earthquake(s)	20, 34, 57, 172, 201
Christchurch, NZ	172
Haiti	172, 201
Eating disorders	124, 126
Economy	
crash	39, 119, 171, 177
crisis	57
Great Depression	39, 56, 63, 196
meltdown	85, 175
recession	11, 15, 39, 46, 152
Wall Street Crash	56
Egypt	67, 164, 225
Elwell, Dennis	27, 198, 207, 218
Employment	88, 90, 100, 102, 117, 121–2, 135, 176, 181
Unemployment	14, 39, 64–5, 71, 90, 121, 184
Endangered species	191
Equality	20, 207, 66, 77, 90–1, 98, 103, 115
Inequality	87–8, 99–100
Euro (currency)	64–5, 69, 226
Europe	40, 46, 64, 65, 71, 163, 172, 201
Evolution	41, 111, 168, 193, 207
Family	7, 11, 29, 41, 47, 60, 73, 115, 206
Farming	39, 48, 72
Foot and mouth	104, 161, 200
Fascism	40
Feminism(/t)	115, 129,143, 203, 208, 218–19
Food	29, 48–9, 73, 126, 138–40, 194, 206
Famine	29, 163
France	28, 64–5, 118, 170, 190
Free will	13
Freedom	20, 22, 24, 28–9, 37, 42, 55, 60, 66, 115, 172–3, 176
Gaddafi, Muammar	28
Gandhi, Mohandas K	40, 205
Gates, Bill	49, 168
Gay Liberation Movement	29
Germany	28–9, 39–40, 64–5, 118

	Nazi	40
Global		29, 45–6, 55, 64, 72, 108, 127, 130, 139–40, 159, 162–3, 170, 182, 235
	(tele)communications	135, 168, 176
	crisis	28, 43, 160
	debt	175
	economy	46, 78, 85, 87, 118, 171–2, 177
	globalization	168
	media	90, 93
	pandemic	200
	population	180
	superpowers	74, 77
	warfare	171
	warming	193
Google		201
Greece		29, 64–5, 68, 121, 225
	Austerity package	64–5

Harry Potter	145–7
Harvey, Charles	12, 25–26, 69, 70, 161, 175, 197, 218,
Health	25, 70, 105, 108, 114–17, 122, 123–33, 138–40, 155, 181, 185–6, 235
National Health Service (NHS)	
	71, 127
Hindus	40
Hitler, Adolf	40, 204
Hotmail	168
Human rights	28–9, 66, 172–3
Human Rights Movement	29, 173
Huxley, Aldous	41

Iceland	43, 79–86, 172, 219, 220, 224
Identity cards	45
Independence movement	28
India	29, 40, 74–6, 205, 225, 227
International Monetary Fund (IMF)	
	49, 64, 69, 226
Internet	42, 45, 106, 108, 159, 162–3, 167–8, 176, 194–5
Intervened births	129, 131
Iraq	170, 179, 201
Iran	164, 171
Irish Republican Army (IRA)	34, 177
Israel	29, 179

Jackson, Michael	34, 154–5, 227
Japan	33, 40, 57, 102, 118, 172, 192, 201
Tokyo	91
Kennedy, John F	28, 33, 88
Kennedy, Robert	173
King Kong	41
King, Martin Luther	33, 88–9, 155, 173, 223
King, Rodney Glenn	94–8, 155, 224
Ku Klux Klan	200
Large Hadron Collider	51
Lawrence, Stephen	99–100
Lehman brothers	74, 83
Libya	28, 67, 224
Limitless	186
Lindbergh, Charles	56, 226
Logan's Run	47
London School of Astrology	102, 205, 231
Mad Cow Disease	104, 161, 200
Madonna	155–6, 227
Malaysia	201
Mandela, Nelson	90–4, 223–224
Mary Poppins	144–5
Medicalization	123, 127, 130
Merriman, Ray	63, 196, 220
Middle East	57, 59, 65, 178, 197
Military	55, 127, 170–1
Mini	152
Monroe, Marilyn	157
Montgomery, Elizabeth	144
Mountbatten, Lord	34
Murdoch, Rupert	60–1
Muslim	40
National	
chart	65–6, 77, 172
grid	171
National Health Service (NHS)	71, 127
National Rail	108
NATO	55, 170

Natural disaster   25, 86, 170, 192
Natural resource   107, 110, 163, 194
New Zealand   33, 91, 172, 180, 192, 230
News of the World, The   60
Nigeria   28, 201
Northern Rock   63

Olympic Games   91, 157
Origin of Species, On The   182
Overpopulation   48

Pakistan   29, 74, 118, 201
Planet of the Apes   33, 41
Pope   34
Popular culture   30, 144, 153
Portugal   38, 65, 68, 145, 225
Presley, Elvis   153, 157
Property   46, 64, 70, 101–2
        market   69, 72, 77, 122, 177
        rights   74
Protest(ers)   28–9, 40, 55–6, 59–60, 65–6, 87–8, 90–1,
                             98–100, 120, 173, 178, 180, 183
Psychotherapy   133, 205

Quantitative easing   107, 171

Racism   88
        Institutionalized   100
Reproductive technologies   32
Revolution(/ary/ize)   20, 24, 29–31, 60–1, 66, 68, 91, 100, 108,
                             138, 153, 208, 225
        Great Proletarian Cultural Revolution
                             29
        Industrial   50–51
        Sexual   115–16, 127
        Social   30
        Technological   61, 105, 127, 135, 163, 207
Rice, Condoleezza   49
Riots   59, 65–6, 87–99, 180
        London   87–8, 164
        Watts   90
        LA   94–100, 224

Rodden, Lois	142, 224
Rowling, JK	145–7, 227
Russia	38
USSR	164
Soviet Union	28, 177
Rwanda	28
Samoa	204
Scandinavia	82, 194
Scholfield, Sy	142, 223
Science fiction	42, 186
Security	29, 49, 102, 107–8, 153, 162–3, 176
job	121
insecurity	170
Service industry	117
Sexual revolution	115–16, 127
Sheldrake, Rupert	189
Siberia	194
Social Science Research Council	141
Sociology	189, 219, 228
Solar system	13, 51, 159
South America	201
Spacecraft	34, 174
Space Race	28
Star Trek	110, 186
Steiner, Rudolph	187–8, 228
Sterilization	40, 124
Stuxnet	171
Sub-prime mortgages	46, 85
Summer of love	29, 115
Superman	56
Sweden	60
Switzerland	49, 52
Syria	67, 225
Tarzan the Ape Man	41
Technological progress	32, 128
Thailand	40
Thames, River	108, 145, 205
Tsunami	57, 85, 172, 191
Tunisia	60, 67, 117, 225
Turkey	28, 230
Twiggy	126, 150–2, 227

United Kingdom (UK)   161, 164, 170-1, 175, 177, 179, 181, 184, 192, 200

    England   50, 58-60, 70, 86, 109, 119-20, 130-1, 137, 145-6, 149, 151, 175, 184-5, 199, 219, 223-4, 226-8

      Northern Ireland   71, 130
      Scotland   71, 125, 130, 227
      Wales   71, 130-1, 149, 219, 227
USA   55-6, 164, 173, 179, 180, 187, 191, 225
      San Francisco   30, 115
      Sibly chart   72-4, 179, 106

Vietnam War   28, 173
Virgin(al)   136, 155-6, 149
      maiden   113-16
      Mary   115
Virgin (Group)   136-8, 173
Volcano(/ic)   85-6, 172
Volkswagen Beetle   152

Warhol, Andy   157
Water shortages   48-9, 107
Wells, HG   42, 221
Wikileaks   60
Wikipedia   42, 159, 167
Witchcraft   143-7
Women's roles   30
Women's suffrage movement   56
Working class   117
World Bank   49
World War   20
      II   201

Xiaobo, Liu   173

Yorkshire Ripper   34
YouTube   159

Zavaroni, Lena   124-5, 227